The Versailles Restaurant Cookbook

UNIVERSITY PRESS OF FLORIDA

Florida A&M University, Tallahassee
Florida Atlantic University, Boca Raton
Florida Gulf Coast University, Ft. Myers
Florida International University, Miami
Florida State University, Tallahassee
New College of Florida, Sarasota
University of Central Florida, Orlando
University of Florida, Gainesville
University of North Florida, Jacksonville
University of South Florida, Tampa
University of West Florida, Pensacola

The Versailles Restaurant Cookbook

ANA QUINCOCES & NICOLE VALLS

Foreword by Andy García

UNIVERSITY PRESS OF FLORIDA

Gainesville · Tallahassee · Tampa · Boca Raton · Pensacola · Orlando · Miami · Jacksonville · Ft. Myers · Sarasota

A Florida Quincentennial Book

22 21 20 19 18 17   7 6 5 4 3 2

Library of Congress Cataloging-in-Publication Data
Quincoces, Ana, author.
The Versailles Restaurant cookbook / Ana Quincoces and
Nicole Valls; foreword by Andy García.
pages cm
Includes index.
ISBN 978-0-8130-4978-6
1. Cooking, Cuban. 2. Cooking—Florida. 3. Cooking, Spanish.
4. Versailles Restaurant—History. I. Valls, Nicole, author.
II. García, Andy. III. Title.
TX716.C8Q46 2014
641.597291—dc23
2014003465

University Press of Florida
15 Northwest 15th Street
Gainesville, FL 32611-2079
http://upress.ufl.edu

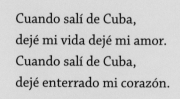

Cuando salí de Cuba,
dejé mi vida dejé mi amor.
Cuando salí de Cuba,
dejé enterrado mi corazón.

—Luis Aguile

What
LO QUE
doesn't kill
NO MATA,
you makes
ENGORDA.
you fatter.

CONTENTS

FOREWORD

Versailles: A Place of Solace

The New Oxford Dictionary's definition of solace is "comfort or consolation in a time of distress or sadness." Solace is not only a state of mind but can also be a place—a place where one finds comfort, consolation, cheer, support, and relief.

All exile communities will find places of solace wherever they end up. Places that provide this most necessary emotional and spiritual space. Where one can gather with fellow exiles and share a profound love and nostalgia for the country they have left. For those of us in the Cuban exile community in Miami, Versailles is such a place.

Since its inception Versailles has been a gathering place not only to reminisce but also to socialize. Its famous "La Ventanita," or small walk-up window, serves you perhaps the most famous and strongest Cuban coffee in the world. Versailles continues to host dignitaries, celebrities, and a constant flow of politicians in need of support as they mingle with the locals. But most important, it is a place where one can immerse oneself in its authentic Cuban culture and vibe.

Its food is exquisite and traditional. The waiters are the real thing, with a joy for life and never without a friendly smile. Its clientele is now of all cultures in need of this experience and great food. And at its heart is that Cuban thing—whether it is the obligatory early morning *café con leche y pan tostado* (coffee with milk and toasted Cuban bread and butter) or an afterhours late night meal to replenish and reconstitute. For me it is white rice with two fried eggs in extra virgin olive oil, sunny side up with fried bananas and *picadillo*, which is a traditional peasant type of ground meat hash.

Memories have been created there by all of us looking for a little something to ease the pain. The hole in one's heart that lives in all exiles who carry with them a deep love for the country left behind. It is like an impossible love. You can love her, but you can't be with her.

But you can find solace somewhere else, and for many, that place is Versailles.

Andy García
Actor/Director/Producer

INTRODUCTION

The History and Family of Versailles

Since 1971 Miami's Little Havana has been home to Versailles Cuban Restaurant. Although Versailles is located in Miami, its origins stem from the Cuban culture and its people. In late 1950s Cuba a political revolution surfaced that resulted in a government takeover by Fidel Castro and his newly formed communist regime. As the rapidly changing Cuban society began to transform from a free society to a communist state, many Cubans fled the island seeking political refuge, with most heading for Miami, Florida. By the 1960s the heart of Cuban Miami was dubbed Little Havana and served as a political haven for the large Cuban community. Among those fleeing was Felipe Valls Sr., a businessman from the province of Santiago de Cuba. He arrived in Miami with his two children, his pregnant wife, a longing for freedom and justice, a craving for *arroz y frijoles*, and his strong belief in the American dream.

Ever the entrepreneur, it wasn't long before Felipe Valls Sr. was making a better life for himself and his family in Miami. A stint selling used restaurant equipment gave Valls an idea that would come to fruition—and has continued to flourish for nearly five decades.

He recognized early on that the ever-expanding Cuban community was longing for a taste of home, a place where transplanted Cubans would find a refuge to congregate and share news from their homeland. A place that would help them both maintain and perpetuate their unique Cuban identity while sipping on a hot freshly brewed Cuban espresso.

From that point on the restless Cuban was all but unstoppable. As his "cafeteria" shop grew in popularity he realized that the next step in capturing the flavors and the essence of his beloved Cuba was to expand his menu and create a more complete Cuban experience via a restaurant.

In 1971 Felipe Valls opened Versailles Restaurant. It marked the onset of fulfilling his vision for a Cuban hub. His goal was to create a place where families could enjoy high quality food at affordable prices. At the time, Little Havana's Calle Ocho had not yet become the bustling business and commerce center it is today. Miami was rapidly increasing in population and diversity, however, and Felipe foresaw this location becoming a central spot in the changing city. The

construction of Versailles on Eighth Street would open up the entire area to the Cuban community and serve as a bridge between the old and new Miami. In the nascent years of its existence, it accommodated only eighty patrons. Once Felipe Jr., son and protégé of Felipe Sr., began to help manage the restaurant, Versailles grew in size and services. Today it accommodates more than four hundred customers and is ever evolving and expanding. Now Versailles is perhaps the most popular and frequented Cuban restaurant anywhere.

If you ask Felipe Sr. or Jr. why their restaurant has maintained its authenticity and clientele, they won't mention the constant media coverage, celebrity customers, or its political significance. They will point to just one factor—and for true restaurateurs, the only important factor—the food.

Felipe Valls opened Versailles with a very simple premise. He wanted his customers to leave happier than when they arrived. He knew that most Cuban immigrants were struggling financially and that restaurant dining was a luxury many of them could not afford. His business model was likewise simple. Provide your patrons with a great meal at a fair price, and they will keep coming back. The restaurant's success still hinges on this premise.

Stuffed green plantains combine classic Cuban ingredients in one perfect bite.

Facing: Detail of lively mural in Miami's Little Havana.

Versailles has continued to grow exponentially, and it is not uncommon for the restaurant to serve a couple of thousand people on any given day. One would think that with its enormous success, Versailles would have been enough of a challenge for Valls. Hardly. Since the opening of Versailles more than four decades ago, the family has opened numerous other equally successful restaurants, continuing their ethos of quality and value at every venue.

While restaurants are notoriously high-risk businesses, it was all but impossible for Versailles to fail. The entire Valls family has a knack for the restaurant business. An uncanny ability never to overlook the minutest detail is the hallmark of the Valls philosophy. At Versailles nothing is ever left to chance. Once a goal is set and attained, it is reset at an even higher level. Impeccable customer service is also an ever-evolving goal of the Valls family. That, coupled with a powerful work

Detail of Calle Ocho tiled mural.

Facing: Diner tabletops balance the etched glass and help customers feel right at home.

ethic and the commitment to treating employees and business associates like family, has made the Valls empire what it is today.

As Valls had hoped, the time and investment spent building and nurturing Versailles paid off. Cuban customers—hungry as much for nostalgia as for food—and the curious Miami locals came in droves. The mass appeal of this Eighth Street restaurant far exceeded his expectations; it drew crowds from all over the globe. Valls acknowledges that the success and the significance of Versailles reflect not only his passion and dedication but also that of his staff, the patrons, and the ever-evolving dynamic city of Miami.

While Versailles is miles away from its namesake, the Château de Versailles in France, both are iconic landmarks in their own ways. There is nary a travel guide or website that fails to mention one or the other as a required stop on any trip to Miami, Florida, or Versailles, France. Versailles, the restaurant, has borrowed some of that French opulence, with gilded mirrors and chandeliers reminiscent of Versailles, the palace, but has combined these with a toned-down diner feel. By incorporating things like vinyl chairs and green plastic bread baskets, the effect is more kitschy than opulent, making patrons feel both special and at home.

More than Just a Restaurant: "La Ventanita"

Versailles is indeed more than just a restaurant. It's a refuge where people come to settle down and relax. To celebrate birthdays and ballet recitals, to grab a late night bite after a big party, and even to be comforted by family and friends after a funeral. For so many of us it is our home away from home. On any given night you will see people in team uniforms or work suits as well as in gowns and tuxedos after an evening out on the town. On Halloween, expect to see a slew of unique,

Pastelito de guayaba sweeten the morning's start.

elaborate, and outrageous costumes at Versailles. It is the place where weary and hungry witches, ghosts, and goblins come to get their *café con leche* and *tostada* after a costume party. These are just some of the things that make Versailles so very special. It has become not only the epicenter and the respite of the exile Cuban community but also a second home and a welcoming beacon to people of every nationality and all walks of life. In this day and age that is more refreshing than a *guarapo* (sugar cane juice) on a smoldering Miami day.

Along one side of Versailles is the even more frequented and media-frenzied coffee window, "La Ventanita." Here *cafecito, croquetas*, and *pastelitos* are enjoyed by the hundreds daily. Versailles brews its own blend of premium espresso, Café La Carreta, which is considered the best *cafecito* in town. The crowd sipping on this ambrosia ranges from old Cuban men discussing politics to young adults getting their caffeine fix before hitting the beach. Countless "Ventanita" visits have been nationally televised and written about. Everyone has graced our little coffee window, from our favorite Hollywood celebrities to community leaders, politicians, and even a few U.S. presidents. For more than forty years and through our famous "Ventanita," our loyal employees have served countless *cafecitos* to the regulars they regard as family and to numerous *famosos* (famous people) who frequent the Calle Ocho establishment. "La Ventanita" is definitely one of the restaurant's most recognizable features. Through the decades it has grown in significance and even attained pop culture status.

Versailles eventually expanded to accommodate the now equally popular Versailles Bakery. The bakery makes all the desserts and pastries for the restaurant. Aside from famously sweet and decadent desserts, the bakery carries all the elements for a typical casual Cuban breakfast. Our loyal morning customers come in for a *cortadito*, a *pastelito*, and a *croqueta*, which they enjoy while sitting in the café reading their copy of *El Nuevo Herald*. They may then stroll to "La Ventanita," where they can discuss the latest news with the other regulars.

Our staff are as diverse as our patrons, and many have been with us since we opened forty years ago. They are more than employees; they are like family, not only to us but to the regulars who confide in and share their stories with the staff. Romance, deal making, politics, gossip, celebrity sightings—it's all in a day's work at this sprawling mirrored gem we call home.

An extension of the Versailles brand is Café Versailles, a Cuban coffee and pastry stand inspired by the "Ventanita" and bakery. There are currently five Café Versailles stands located at the Miami International Airport. Our loyal customers love being able to enjoy their *cortaditos*, *croquetas*, *pastelitos*, or sandwiches while they are at the airport, or even better, take some with them on their journey.

Cafecito for one and all.

Politics with a Side of Plantains

Versailles is an institution and landmark that is often referred to by locals as the "Cuban Embassy." It stands as a beacon for free speech and democracy and lovingly embraces all cultures. A visit from the Dalai Lama served as a beautiful and spiritual stamp of approval.

For more than forty years Versailles has been ground zero for the Cuban community to get their caffeine fix, reminisce about the Cuba of yesteryear, and plot the fall of Fidel Castro. Whether in the ornate dining room or outside at "La Ventanita," Versailles is a place where Cubans of every stripe congregate to vent about work, politics, and life in general.

It wasn't long after opening its doors in 1971 that Versailles became the unofficial town square for Miami's transplanted Cubans. It should come as no surprise that politicians stop here to rally the support of the ever-loyal Cuban community. The media are aware of how much a group of Cubans outside Versailles sharing a *colada* can register the sentiment of the entire Cuban community. Many a campaign has been at least slanted in one direction or another on Versailles' politically hallowed ground.

Versailles has been the site of many peaceful demonstrations as well as uproarious celebrations. When rumors surfaced that Fidel Castro had died, people flocked to the restaurant in droves to confirm the story and to celebrate the possibility that it might be true. When the Miami Heat wins championships, people take to the streets surrounding Versailles equipped with pots and pans and celebrate their team's victory noisily into the wee hours.

A less happy occasion—and one that left an indelible mark in the hearts and minds of many Miamians, including the Valls family—was the deportation of Elián González. The saga of Elián González caused an insurmountable rift between the Hispanic community and the immigration and law enforcement authorities that is to some extent palpable even today. It is difficult not to be haunted by the image of that little boy hiding in a closet when overly armed law enforcement agents came to yank him from the arms of the family who had embraced him so completely. It was heart wrenching, as all of us in Miami and perhaps the entire country had fallen in love with Elián and suffered his plight along with him. Some even surmise that the Elián debacle affected the outcome of the 2000 presidential election, since both Al Gore and George W. Bush weighed in on the matter, dividing a nation on the issue of immigration.

Local and national media are often seen outside Versailles. They know it is the best place to get contrasting points of view from real people—those out in the trenches of the workplace, retired folks, stay-at-home moms, students, you name it. The diversity of the people who frequent Versailles is really quite surprising.

Rudy Giuliani enjoying his morning *cafecito* at "La Ventanita."

Cuban coffee in life and art.

Pastelitos and *croquetas* go well with news of the day.

Jeb Bush, Felipe Valls Sr., and George W. Bush.

It is not surprising, however, that year after year both local and national politicians flock to Versailles, many promising the patrons toughness on Fidel Castro and reformation of immigration policies. They are aware of what it takes to garner the support of the Hispanic community, and this is the best place to do so.

Presidential candidates, especially, know that Florida is a crucial battleground and that the Hispanic vote can sometimes make or break an election. Presidents Ronald Reagan, George H. W. Bush, George W. Bush, and Bill Clinton have all enjoyed Cuban delicacies and a few *cafecitos* at Versailles. We have been privileged to serve many important political figures and presidential hopefuls such as Hillary Clinton, John McCain, Paul Ryan, and Mitt Romney. People like Jeb Bush, Rick Scott, Rudy Giuliani, Charlie Crist, Mel Martinez, and of course our Miami mayors are practically regulars. But mostly our customers consist of the local community, with a blend of curious tourists from all over the world. It is this core customer base that has made Versailles a Miami institution.

Cultural Heroes

Versailles endures by serving quality food and thrives on the diversity of its people. It is especially enhanced by the clients as well as the cultural influencers and artists who enjoy the Cuban cuisine and the ambiance here.

Any time a famous actor, rock star, or professional athlete stops by Versailles, we are reminded that good food brings people of all kinds together. Over the years we have served many talented people, such as Willy Chirino, Olga Guillot, Julio and Enrique Iglesias, Jay Z, Beyoncé, Gloria and Emilio Estefan, the Beach Boys, Pitbull, Robert Duvall, John Stamos, Carlos Vives, Juanes, Kate Hudson, Eduardo Verástegui, Nina Dobrev, Olga Tañón, Roselyn Sánchez, Christian Slater, Celia Cruz, Cachao, Luis Fonsi, Alejandra Guzmán, Ana María Polo, Lili Estefan, María Elena Salinas, Pamela Silva, Perez Hilton, Rufus Wainwright, Rodner Figueroa, Raúl Molina, Mike Lowell, Sammy Sosa, El Duque and Liván Hernández, and Chris Bosh, to name only a few. Of course many wonderful chefs frequent Versailles as well. People like Art Smith, Bobby Flay, Jose Andres, Aarón Sánchez, Daniel Boulud, Lorena Garcia, Andrew Zimmern, and Sunny Anderson make it a point to stop by when they need their Cuban fix.

The Backbone of Our Business

A restaurant like Versailles could never have survived four decades without help from many people. The Valls family has always considered everyone who walked into this gilded, mirrored home away from home to be family. Whether they work at Versailles bussing tables, waiting on guests, managing a shift or are customers just stopping by to get their morning or afternoon *cafecito*, these people are the essence of Versailles.

Take the "teenagers," for example. They are actually about eight to twelve Santiagueros, Cuban men from Santiago de Cuba, ranging in age from their mid-sixties to late seventies. They congregate in the area called the "salon de los espejos," or room of mirrors. These men have had lunch at Versailles Monday through Friday since the day it opened—yes, that's right, almost every day of the week for more than forty years. We're talking about more than ten thousand visits! That's a lot of *lechón asado* (roast pork).

Curious as to what brought them to the same establishment day after day, we joined them for lunch one afternoon. They were surprised to be asked, "Why the same place, same people, every day?" Their reaction made us feel a little foolish and insensitive to the cherished time they spend together. Most are from the same province in Cuba as Felipe Sr. Several in this group of Cuban men and a few stragglers (who they joke have to apply for a special visa to sit with them) have known one another since their childhood in Santiago de Cuba. In Cuba they attended a Jesuit school called Dolores, and their friendship has endured adolescence, relocation, adulthood, marriages, divorces, children, grandchildren, and Castro—a subject that still hangs over them like a dark cloud of melancholy. They have provided comfort and joy to one another in the face of their difficult past.

Furthermore, very few restaurants can boast of having employees for forty plus years. Zoraida, the waitress everyone knows as "Tía," has called Versailles

home for more than four decades. Tía has been around since Versailles opened and considers herself an extension of the Valls family. She proudly states that her most prized possession is the wooden plaque Felipe Jr. and Sr. presented to her to commemorate her thirty years of excellent service at Versailles. It is displayed in the center of her living room. Tía is now eighty years old and recently had to retire following knee surgery. When asked if she had anything to say to readers, she replied, "Los días más felices de mi vida los pasé en el Versailles" (The happiest moments of my life were my days at Versailles).

Another longtime employee is Max, who managed the waiters and busboys for years with a swift hand and familial smile. He was personally brought on by Felipe Jr. after working with him in other Valls family–owned restaurants. This Galician is a man of few words who relishes hard work in the name of good food and enjoys the restaurant most when it is busiest. His favorite indulgence is the *sopa de pollo* (chicken soup), which he eats daily and tops with a spoonful of white rice.

The success of Versailles hinges upon the wonderful employees who have graced the establishment for so many years. Versailles owners and customers will be forever grateful to hardworking individuals like Tía and Max who have made the restaurant the warm and special place that it is today.

We have been fortunate enough to have Tony Piedra as part of the Versailles family for more than thirty-three years now. Tony serves as Versailles' corporate executive chef, but he is so much more than that. This Spanish-born dynamo is the first to remind you that he is no typical culinary school graduate. Sure, he is classically trained, but his experience growing up surrounded by chefs (his father and brother are both chefs in Spain), and training in restaurants all over Europe, have made Tony the passionate culinary genius that he is today.

Tony's vast experience and discriminating palate have influenced the minutest details of the Versailles menu. And while Cuban food is pretty simple fare, it is deeply rooted in the complex flavors and traditions of Spanish cuisine.

Tony's unique perspective has influenced everything from the procurement of the freshest and local (when possible) ingredients to the procedures used by the staff to break down meats and produce, and in searing and braising, and even the order in which the vegetables are added to a stew at just the right time. No detail is ever overlooked by this talented, multilingual chef, who also happens to be quite a character. The success of Versailles has so much to do with the talented group of individuals we are lucky enough to work with every single day, many of them for decades now. Tony is certainly at the top of that list.

Facing: The loyal employees and staff epitomize the spirit of Versailles.

The Founding Father: Felipe Valls Sr.

Fearless is the best word to describe Felipe Valls Sr. We often hear stories of Cuban immigrants who leave the deplorable conditions in Cuba for a better life in the United States; however, that wasn't exactly Felipe's story. While he did not want to live under the oppression of communism, Felipe and his family were anything but destitute. Felipe had attended Riverside Military Academy, a preparatory boarding school in the United States. He returned to Cuba equipped with the English language and an innate business savvy and became a very successful businessman. He owned a slew of businesses including gas stations, restaurants, and even an auto parts distribution operation. He opened a large plant that manufactured paper bags for the cement industry and was in the process of building an iron ore processing plant with the well-known German company Krupps when he left his beloved Cuba. Valls dabbled in the bottling business as well, providing bottles to numerous important liquor companies like Bacardi® and Hatuey®. As if all this weren't enough, he also had a restaurant equipment company and imported espresso machines from abroad. Who knew that Valls would serve enough coffee in his lifetime to fill a small country?

Hundreds of customers flow through Versailles each hour to enjoy the cuisine.

But despite his enormous success and entrepreneurship in the country of his birth, Valls was forced to leave it all behind, finding himself, like many immigrants, jobless and penniless in a foreign country. He eventually found a job where he was able to put some of his skills to work. His first job in Miami was working for a restaurant supply company. In true Valls form he parlayed this experience into opening his own company importing espresso machines from Europe and selling them, along with air conditioners and refrigeration equipment, to numerous local restaurants. Once Valls transitioned into the actual restaurant business, there was no stopping him. He started with Badia Restaurant in Little Havana, followed by Versailles.

Chandeliers elevate the atmosphere in the Versailles dining room.

Valls knew he had a knack for business, but even he never imagined that his modest restaurant would become the iconic landmark it is today, serving a couple of thousand hungry patrons per day.

Later Valls and his namesake son, Felipe Jr., opened the now famous La Carreta chain of Cuban restaurants. Currently the Valls Group has more than two thousand employees at their many restaurants and cafés around Miami-Dade and Broward counties as well as numerous food outlets at the Miami International Airport.

Valls is truly a shining example of the remarkable economic success of Cubans in this country. He has been dubbed the "Cuban Midas," referencing the golden touch with which he anoints all his businesses. Everything Valls touches seems to turn to gold. Be it through hard work, tenacity, business acumen, luck, or a combination of all these, Valls is an emblematic figure in the Cuban community and an inspiration to all immigrants.

He resides in Miami with his family. Although he longs to visit his beloved Cuba, he has yet to return due to the political climate there. He continues to visit Versailles every single day. He is as active in the day-to-day operations as he ever was. Valls believes there is plenty of time to rest when his time on this planet comes to an end. In the meantime, there is little he can do to stop his brain from working overtime. We suspect that will be the case for years to come. Valls considers himself truly fortunate to have his son, Felipe Valls Jr., as his partner. Felipe has helped turn his father's vision into a veritable empire, as have his sisters, daughters, nephews, and nieces, who have all contributed greatly to the success and legacy of the Valls family.

Like Father Like Son

The only son of Felipe Valls Sr., Felipe began working with his father at the ripe old age of thirteen. When most other kids his age were watching television or playing with their friends, Felipe was working in construction, building the family restaurants. He learned the restaurant business from the ground up and remained in that capacity until he was seventeen years old. And as if his hard labor at the weekday job were not enough, Felipe worked at the restaurant on weekends as well. But don't think Felipe was bossing people around, behaving like the entitled heir. In an effort to teach his son the work ethic that was necessary to take over the family business someday, Felipe Sr. decided his son would start at the bottom—way bottom! And what did that entail? Washing dishes, of course. Felipe Jr. washed dishes until he proved himself worthy and responsible enough to hold the prestigious position of busboy. For several years Felipe Jr. was either washing dirty dishes or clearing them. Talk about tough love.

Years later Felipe had earned his way into the kitchen, where he worked as head of the line for more than five years. Felipe credits his dishwasher, busboy,

Three generations proud: Felipe Valls Jr., Felipe Valls Sr., and Nicole Valls.

and head of the line days for making him a better boss. Having actually done the work employees do every single day afforded him a greater appreciation of the kind of effort that goes into those jobs, an understanding that has made him a more humane and empathetic employer.

Felipe attended Florida International University, where he studied business and majored in finance. FIU has one of the top hospitality schools in the country, and Felipe considered that major, but with so much hands-on experience at the family restaurants, he stuck with business and graduated with a bachelor's degree in finance.

The business degree has served him well. After graduating from college he opened El Cid, a high end Spanish cuisine restaurant, followed by Copacabana, a lounge and supper club, and the second of several La Carreta restaurants. Felipe oversees all aspects of the restaurant business, from location scouting, concept creation, food, liquor, and design layout to construction, staff hiring, and managing the day-to-day operations. Despite his enormous responsibility, Felipe has continued to open restaurants at a clip of about one per year.

Today the Valls Group owns and operates dozens of restaurants in South Florida. Not bad for the boy who washed dishes. Felipe credits his father in large part for his work ethic and for always making him feel an equal partner in the family business. He never felt like an employee. He proudly says that his father never held him back, always considered his input, and most surprisingly, never butted heads with him. He says the transition was subtle and did not involve a ceremonial passing of the torch. He simply started taking over more and more responsibilities until one day, before he knew it, he was in charge. But that kind of independence came at a stiff price, and Felipe recalls working eighteen-hour days, six days a week, for many years. He also remembers his father asking his senior employees to give his then young son "the hardest jobs available." That kind of approach, Felipe Jr. believes, was instrumental in helping him become the highly respected business professional he is today. And while he has created a small empire, it has taken decades, sacrifice, and discipline to reach that point. For more than twenty-five years the family diligently reinvested all their profits back into the business. Only in recent years have they decided to enjoy the well-deserved fruits of their labor.

Felipe lives in Miami with his wife, Lourdes. They have six daughters, some living at home and others away at college. Felipe is a family man through and through and enjoys nothing more than relaxing at home or traveling with his family.

If you cook

Si cocinas como

like you walk

caminas hasta la

I'll eat every

raspa me como.

last bite.

SOME BASICS

The wonderful thing about Cuban cuisine is the sheer simplicity of it. Those who are not familiar with this cuisine assume that cooking Cuban food is a complicated undertaking. Nothing could be further from the truth. Cuban food is unbelievably flavorful, not necessarily spicy, but savory and brimming with bold flavors that delight the palate. So how can food be so delicious but also simple to make? It's the holy trinity, of course! Don't worry; it's not a religious thing and converting is not required, although some people consider that a really good Cuban meal is tantamount to a religious experience. Well—that may be a slight exaggeration. But when you grew up on this stuff, nothing beats it—nothing!

So what is this holy trinity? It's the delectable combination of garlic, yellow onion, and bell pepper. These three elements combined are the foundation of Cuban cuisine and the main ingredients in our ever-popular *sofrito*. So it is no surprise that *sofrito* is the first recipe in this book. At Versailles or at any Cuban restaurant worth its salt, a well-made *sofrito* sets the stage for the entire recipe. And while making a *sofrito* is simple, it does require a little kitchen elbow grease. A little chopping, a little stirring, and some love goes a long way in making this important step of every Cuban meal a success.

Another very important component of the Cuban pantry is *mojo*. *Mojo* is Cuba's answer to ketchup. It's delicious on almost everything. We venture to suggest there are few things that could not be improved by being topped with or dipped in a little *mojo*. Traditionally *mojo* is made using sour oranges. Sour oranges are kind of bumpy and thick skinned, with a highly acidic juice that lends itself perfectly to a marinade or dipping sauce. Sour oranges are not always available, and because they are full of seeds and dry out easily, they do not render much juice. At Versailles, rather than using sour orange, grapefruit juice and lime are combined to mimic the level of acidity and minimal sweetness that sour oranges provide. Feel free to use either to make your *mojo*. Use this *mojo* on all your favorite meats and to dip your plantain chips and *tostones* (see glossary). The versatility of *mojo* is such that once you make it, you'll wonder how you managed to cook and eat without it.

Throughout the recipes you will often see "salt and pepper to taste" in the ingredients. Cuban food is not spicy, but it is flavorful and very tasty. We believe it is imperative to taste test everything before you serve it to friends and family. Adjusting the salt and pepper can make or break a dish. Things like stock and canned sauces contribute to the sodium in a dish quite dramatically, so when we call for a specific amount of salt, it is usually the minimum amount.

Honeymooning in Miami with Versailles

My wife Jody and I were married in April of 2006, and we spent our honeymoon in Miami. While there we discovered Versailles on Calle Ocho and fell in love with it. We spent quite a few meals there savoring the flavors of the food, atmosphere, and the people. We loved it so much that when we returned to Miami for our second trip, the first place we went after we landed was Versailles. Versailles is in our blood and there is not a week that goes by that we don't talk about Versailles and dream about returning.
—Hershel Martin

Basic Tomato-Based Sauce ◈ Sofrito

Sofrito is the foundation of many Cuban dishes. It is also a wonderful condiment, especially with store-bought roast chicken or sautéed mushrooms. This *sofrito* can be stored in the refrigerator for up to 5 days in a tightly sealed container.

Makes about 2 cups

¼ cup olive oil
1 large onion, chopped
4 garlic cloves, minced
1 medium green bell pepper, chopped
1 cup crushed tomatoes
1 bay leaf
¼ cup *vino seco* (dry white cooking wine)
1 teaspoon salt
½ teaspoon pepper
½ teaspoon dried oregano
½ teaspoon ground cumin

◈ Heat the olive oil in a large frying pan over medium heat. Add the onion, garlic, and bell pepper, and sauté until the onion is translucent, 5 to 7 minutes. Add the tomatoes, bay leaf, and *vino seco*, and cook 5 minutes more. Reduce the heat to low, add the salt, pepper, oregano, and cumin, and stir. Cover the pan and let the vegetables simmer for 10 to 15 minutes. Remove and discard the bay leaf.

Mojo Criollo

½ cup olive oil
10 to 12 garlic cloves, minced
1 medium yellow onion, grated
2 teaspoons salt
½ teaspoon white pepper
¾ cup sour orange juice, or a mixture of equal parts lime juice and grapefruit juice

◈ Heat the oil in a medium saucepan over medium-low heat. Add the garlic, onion, salt, and pepper and sauté for 10 to 15 minutes. Remove from the heat and add the sour orange juice or the lime/grapefruit juice combination. Set aside to cool to room temperature.

Note: The *mojo* will keep for up to a week, covered and refrigerated.

Hungrier

PASAN MÁS

than a rat in

HAMBRE QUE

a hardware

UN RATÓN EN

store.

FERRETERÍA.

APPETIZERS

Our culture loves to *picar* (nibble). Appetizers or starters are rarely served individually at the dinner table but rather are passed around in large platters while family members grab handfuls of the treats, fearing that the plate won't come around a second time. Our appetizer section comprises the most popular "sharable" plates at Versailles. These are the dishes people not only share before their meal but also eat late at night in lieu of a meal. In essence they are Cuban "bar food," for lack of a better term.

Everyone has a favorite appetizer or snack at Versailles. There is scarcely a time when the waiter arrives at the table to take drink orders (with a green basket of hot buttery bread in hand, mind you) without members of the group starting to call out their favorite starters to share, tapas style. Going to Versailles is often a group activity. Whether you go before or after a function, in your team uniform, or in black tie, Versailles is a must stop to fill the void in your belly that only good Cuban food can satisfy. So whether it's *mariquitas con mojo*—freshly and delicately fried plantain strips with garlic sauce (Cuban ketchup, as we like to call it)—or creamy, delectable chicken or ham *croquetas*, or our popular *yuquitas fritas* with cilantro aioli, you are in for a real treat.

Sometimes patrons come in and order every appetizer on the menu, and then the feeding frenzy begins. Yes, it gets loud sometimes, but that is the wonderful thing about Versailles. Food is made to be shared and enjoyed while exchanging stories and telling the latest Pepito joke (the Cuban equivalent of "little Johnny"). Versailles brings families together, and appetizers are often the precursor to a fabulous meal, which is almost certainly followed by a few shared desserts and then languishing over your *cortadito* or *cafecito*.

The recipes here tease your palate but can also satisfy a big appetite. We are not talking about cheese and crackers. These appetizers are hot and flavorful, with a few exceptions that are served cold. There is something for everyone in this chapter. Salty, crunchy, spicy, creamy, tangy—you name it. So, let's get started! These appetizer recipes epitomize the joy of Cuban cuisine and are sure to become favorites.

Plantain Chips ◈ Mariquitas with Mojo Criollo

Who needs chips and salsa when you can feast on these crispy strips of heaven? Few things can compare to a fresh-from-the-fryer plantain chip dipped in garlic *mojo*. Eating just one is an absolute impossibility, so make plenty—they go fast!

Serves 4 to 6

2 or 3 green plantains
3 cups vegetable oil
sea salt

◈ Heat the oil to 375°F in a large, heavy pot over medium-high heat.

Once the oil is hot, peel a plantain and cut into paper-thin slices, no more than 1/16 of an inch thick. Immediately place the slices into the hot oil and fry the plantains for 3 to 4 minutes, turning them occasionally, until they are crisp but not brown. Transfer the fried plantains to drain on a paper towel–lined plate and sprinkle them generously with salt.

Let the oil return to 375°F before cutting more slices and frying each consecutive batch.

Mojo Criollo for Mariquitas

10 to 12 garlic cloves, minced
1 teaspoons salt
½ teaspoon white pepper
¼ cup grapefruit juice
¼ cup fresh lime juice
1 tablespoon white vinegar
1 bay leaf
3 tablespoons of water or more to
   reduce acidity

◈ Combine all the ingredients and mix well. Taste, adding more salt and water as necessary. Allow to sit for 30 minutes to an hour before serving alongside hot mariquitas (plantain chips).

Note: This *mojo* is uncooked and is generally used for fried vegetables. It will keep for up to a week, covered and refrigerated.

Ham, Chicken, or Cod Croquettes ◈ Croquetas de Jamón, Pollo, o Bacalao

Croquetas are probably everyone's favorite Cuban snack food. They are certainly popular at Versailles. *Croquetas* are fried little bundles of goodness and everyone loves them. They are a little time-consuming to make but well worth the effort. These are great alone, in a sandwich, or with any meal. With so many fillings to choose from, you will never tire of eating them.

Although *croquetas* are perfectly acceptable at room temperature, they are best right out of the fryer—crispy on the outside, creamy and divine on the inside. These little treats are so flexible; they can be made in large quantities and frozen until ready to fry. So there's no reason why you should have to save these for parties or special occasions.

Serve them with our delightful Ensalada de Pollo, page 61.

Ham Croquettes ◇ Croquetas de Jamón

Makes 25 to 30

2 cups whole milk
1 stick of salted butter
½ cup all-purpose flour
½ teaspoon salt or more to taste
½ teaspoon ground nutmeg
½ teaspoon ground white pepper
3 cups ground sweet deli ham (you can
   buy it sliced from the deli and pulse it
   in a food processor until finely ground)
2 cups ground cracker meal or bread
   crumbs
3 eggs, beaten
oil for frying

Chicken Croquettes ◇ Croquetas de Pollo

The only difference between the chicken and ham croquettes is that you will be using cooked ground chicken instead of ham. Use a combination of white and dark roasted skinless chicken meat, and pulse it in your food processor until finely ground. In addition, increase the salt by 1 or 1½ teaspoons, since the chicken is less salty than the ham.

◇ The base of this recipe is a thick béchamel sauce. In a heavy saucepan, bring the milk to a boil. In a separate large saucepan, melt the butter until it begins to bubble. Whisk in the flour, salt, nutmeg, and pepper. Reduce the heat to low and continue stirring until the flour mixture attains a light golden color. While continuing to whisk, add milk a cup at a time, incorporating each addition completely before adding the next. Once all the milk has been added, bring heat up to medium and bring to a boil. Continue stirring to avoid getting large lumps. Once the béchamel has thickened, add the ground ham and combine well. Set aside and allow the mixture to come to room temperature, then refrigerate for at least 4 hours.

In two separate bowls, place the cracker meal and the beaten eggs. Take about an ounce or a heaping tablespoon of ham mixture at a time and form it into cylinders about 1 inch in diameter and 2 inches long. Dip each cylinder in egg and then roll in cracker meal. Do this twice with each cylinder. Allow the *croquetas* to rest refrigerated for about an hour before frying.

Heat about 3 inches of oil in a large frying pan to 375°F over medium-high heat. Fry the *croquetas* until golden brown on all sides. Do not fry too many at once, and allow the oil to regain the original temperature before adding the next batch. Drain on paper towels. Serve with saltine crackers and a squeeze of lime or in a Croqueta Preparada (see recipe, page 130).

Note: Did you know our ham croquettes are one of Versailles' most sought after recipes?

Cod Croquettes ◈ Croquetas de Bacalao

Makes 20 to 25

12 ounces salt cod soaked for at least
   4 hours and rinsed well
2 tablespoons olive oil
½ cup onion, finely minced
2 cloves garlic, minced
3 tablespoons minced parsley
2 cups whole milk
3 tablespoons butter
4–5 tablespoons flour
salt and white pepper
2 cups cracker meal
2 eggs, slightly beaten
light olive oil for frying

*No se puede tapar el
sol con un dedo.*

It is impossible to cover
the sun with one finger.

◈ Drain the cod and flake into small
pieces. In a large skillet heat the olive oil
over medium heat. Add the onion and
garlic and cook for 5 to 7 minutes, until
the onion is translucent. Add the cod
and parsley and cook for an additional 3
to 4 minutes.

In a medium saucepan bring milk to a
boil. In a separate large saucepan, melt
the butter over medium heat. Whisk
in the flour and cook for 3 minutes,
stirring continuously. Add the hot milk
little by little while whisking continuously. Add the pepper. Taste the sauce
and add salt as necessary. Continue
whisking until sauce has thickened. Mix
the cod with the béchamel and allow it
to come to room temperature. Refrigerate for at least 4 hours or overnight.

In two separate bowls, place the cracker
meal and the beaten eggs. Take about
an ounce or a heaping tablespoon of the
cod mixture at a time and form it into
cylinders about 1 inch in diameter and 2
inches long. Dip each cylinder in egg and
then roll in cracker meal. Do this twice
with each cylinder. Allow the *croquetas*
to rest refrigerated for about an hour
before frying.

Heat about 3 inches of oil in a large frying pan to 375°F over medium-high heat.
Fry the *croquetas* until golden brown on
all sides. Do not fry too many at once
and allow the oil to regain the original
temperature before adding the next
batch. Drain on paper towels. Serve with
saltine crackers and a squeeze of lime.

Codfish Fritters ◈ Frituras de Bacalao

Cod fritters are a delicious way to get the party started. These bite-size treats are easy to eat and great for serving at parties. The savory fish batter is the perfect companion to an ice cold beer. Try them with a dash of hot sauce!

Serves 6 to 8

1 pound salt cod
4 large eggs, beaten
6 tablespoons all-purpose flour
1 teaspoon baking powder
3 tablespoons grated white onion
2 tablespoons diced parsley
¼ teaspoon white pepper
½ teaspoon sweet paprika
2 to 3 cups vegetable oil for frying
hot sauce, for serving
lime wedges, for serving

◈ Place the cod in a large bowl and add enough water to cover. Soak the cod for at least 10 to 12 hours, changing the water frequently. Place the cod in a large pot and add enough water to cover. Bring to a boil and boil for 1 hour over medium-high heat, adding more water as necessary. Transfer the cod to a plate and set aside to cool. Pick out any bones from the cod, then chop it finely. Set aside.

Combine the eggs, flour, baking powder, onion, parsley, pepper, and sweet paprika in a large bowl and mix well. Add the cod and mix until it is fully incorporated into the batter. In a large heavy pot, heat 2 to 3 inches of oil to about 375°F over medium-high heat. Drop the batter by heaping tablespoons into the hot oil; the fritters should puff up a little. Fry for about 4 minutes total, turning the fritters when the edges look golden, after about 2 minutes. Transfer the fritters to a paper towel–lined plate and serve immediately with hot sauce and lime wedges.

Malanga Fritters ◆ Frituras de Malanga

Malanga fritters are similar to the consistency and style of cod fritters. Malanga, like yuca, is another Caribbean root vegetable. It looks like a cousin of the potato and is prepared in similar ways. This brown-skinned, white-fleshed vegetable turns slightly gray when boiled and beautifully golden brown when fried, as in this recipe.

Serves 6 to 8

2 cups peeled and cubed malanga,
   boiled for 3 minutes and cooled
2 large eggs
1 garlic clove, minced
3 tablespoons minced sweet onion
1 teaspoon salt
½ teaspoon white pepper
½ teaspoon sweet paprika
2 tablespoons all-purpose flour
2 to 3 cups canola oil

◆ Combine the malanga, eggs, garlic, onion, salt, pepper, paprika, and flour in a food processor or blender and blend well. The batter should be thick.

Heat about 2 inches of oil in a large frying pan over medium-high heat. Drop the batter by heaping tablespoons into the hot oil; the fritters should puff up a little. Fry for about 4 minutes, turning the fritters when the edges look golden, after about 2 minutes. Transfer the fritters to a paper towel–lined plate and serve immediately.

Haz bien y no mires a quien.

Do good and don't worry about anybody else.

Fried Yuca with Cilantro Aioli Dipping Sauce ◆ Yuca Frita con Salsa de Cilantro

If you love French fries, try this unique vegetable fried. You will love the crisp exterior and the tender creamy center. Of course, the cilantro dipping sauce (which is also great with *croquetas*) is reason enough to make these.

If you've never had yuca (a popular Hispanic root vegetable, often called yucca in English), try this version first. It is a unique substitute for French fries and has a mild flavor everyone loves. Make an extra batch of sauce, though—double dipping is the norm!

Serves 4 to 6

1 tablespoon salt
1 tablespoon white vinegar
Approximately 3 pounds frozen
   or fresh yuca
oil for frying

◈ Bring a large pot of water to a boil. Add salt and vinegar. Boil peeled yuca for about 45 to 50 minutes, until tender. Let yuca cool and dry completely.

Cut the yuca into 2-inch-thick strips and deep fry in oil at 350°F. Sprinkle with salt and serve with Cilantro Aioli sauce.

Cilantro Aioli ◆ Salsa de Cilantro

1 bunch fresh cilantro
¼ cup fresh lemon juice
3 tablespoons water
½ cup minced garlic
1 teaspoon salt
1 teaspoon black pepper
2 cups mayonnaise, homemade or store
   bought

◈ Mix together all the ingredients except the mayo. Blend the ingredients using a hand blender until a fine purée forms, about 3 minutes. Combine with the mayonnaise. Add salt and additional pepper if necessary.

Versailles®

Ceviche

Ceviche is a light and fresh white fish salad marinated in citrus juice. This Peruvian dish has made its way to the Cuban table, and the Versailles version is especially good. It is the perfect light meal for summer days—or almost any day in Miami—and can be paired with a crunchy side such as Versailles' homemade malanga chips.

Serves 4 to 6

2 pounds very fresh white fish cut into strips

2 jalapeños finely minced

½ cup finely chopped cilantro

¾ cup fresh squeezed lime juice

¼ cup fresh squeezed orange juice

1 teaspoon salt

Garnish

red onion slices

diced tomatoes

sliced avocado

◈ Combine all ingredients except red onion slices, diced tomato, and avocado in large bowl. Allow to sit for 45 minutes to an hour depending on size of fish strips. Add more salt and pepper if necessary. Garnish with sliced red onion, avocado, and diced tomatoes. Serve with fried boniato (sweet potato) or malanga chips.

Beef Turnovers ◆ Empanadas de Carne

Empanadas are not only a Cuban staple but a common treat in many Hispanic and Latino cultures because they are versatile, easy to eat, and delicious. Beef empanadas are one of the most popular and are made using *picadillo* (meat hash). Obviously, leftover *picadillo* is the perfect excuse to fry up some empanadas. Empanada options are endless—from this savory beef recipe to the uniquely Cuban combination of guava and cream cheese, you can eat them for breakfast, lunch, dinner, and dessert!

Makes 20

¼ cup olive oil

4 garlic cloves, minced

1 medium onion, chopped

1 small green bell pepper, minced

1 pound ground sirloin or ground round

¼ cup *vino seco* (dry white cooking wine)

½ cup crushed tomatoes

½ cup low-sodium chicken stock

½ teaspoon dried oregano

1 bay leaf

1 teaspoon ground cumin

salt and pepper to taste

¼ cup raisins

¼ cup pimiento-stuffed olives, roughly chopped

2 packages of frozen empanada disks (thawed in refrigerator)

vegetable oil for frying

◆ To make the *picadillo* filling, heat half the olive oil in a medium-sized shallow pot over medium-high heat. Add the garlic, onion, and bell pepper, and sauté for 5 to 7 minutes, until tender. Raise the heat slightly. Add the beef when the pan is hot and sauté, breaking up any large chunks of meat. Sauté for 10 to 15 minutes, until the beef is thoroughly cooked (no longer red). Drain any excess liquid from the pan.

Add the *vino seco*, crushed tomato, chicken stock, the remaining olive oil, oregano, bay leaf, ground cumin, and salt and pepper to taste. Reduce the heat to low, cover the pot, and simmer for about 20 minutes. Add the raisins and olives. Allow the *picadillo* to cool before filling the empanada disks.

On a flat surface place thawed but cold empanada disks and add 1½–2 tablespoons *picadillo* on one side of the circle, leaving an inch of edge. Fold the other side over the *picadillo* to make a half moon. Seal using the tines of a fork, making sure that the edges are completely closed. Repeat until all disks are used.

Heat oil to medium-high in a large skillet. Carefully fry the empanadas 2–3 minutes per side, turning only once, until golden brown. Drain on paper towel.

Note: The above quantities will make one pound of *picadillo* filling.

Stuffed Green Plantains ◈ Tostones Rellenos

As if *tostones*—fried green plantains—weren't already divine on their own, we have gone and stuffed them! I recommend these when you are serving something light. But they can certainly stand alone as a main course.

Serves 6 to 8

6 slices of canned pineapple

¼ cup olive oil

½ cup onion, finely diced

¼ cup green bell pepper, finely diced

2 garlic cloves, finely minced

¾ cup crushed tomatoes

¼ teaspoon crushed red pepper flakes

pinch of ground cumin

¼ cup *vino seco* (dry white cooking wine)

salt and pepper to taste

1 pound medium shrimp, peeled and deveined

Approximately 12 to 16 freshly fried *tostones* (page 137)

¼ cup cilantro, finely chopped

Sigue acabando con la quinta y con los mangos.

You are finishing with the farm and the mangos.*

*You are wreaking havoc.

◈ Place the pineapple slices in a hot nonstick skillet and cook over medium-high heat until golden brown, about 3 minutes per side. Cut into ½-inch pieces and set aside.

Heat 3 tablespoons of the oil in the same skillet and add the onion and bell pepper. Cook for about 3 minutes and add the garlic. Continue cooking for 3 minutes more.

Add the tomatoes and spices and continue cooking an additional 7 to 8 minutes. Add the wine and salt and pepper to taste and continue cooking for an additional 3 minutes. Remove from heat and set aside. In a separate skillet, heat the remaining oil over medium-high heat. Season the shrimp with salt and pepper. Add shrimp and reserved pineapple and cook, stirring frequently, until the shrimp are opaque, 2 to 3 minutes. Add shrimp and pineapple to the tomato mixture and continue cooking for 2 or 3 minutes more. Adjust seasoning if necessary. Top freshly fried *tostones* with 1 to 1½ tablespoons of this shrimp mixture, depending on the size of the *tostón*. Garnish with chopped cilantro and serve immediately.

Note: You may be able to find premade frozen *tostones* cups in the Hispanic section of your grocer's freezer.

Santiago-Style Chicken Pie ◈ Pastelón de Pollo Santiaguero

The *pastel de pollo* is the Cuban version of chicken pot pie, and Versailles chefs can barely make it fast enough. When it is oven fresh and ready to sell, it flies like . . . well, *pastel de pollo*. It has taken Versailles years to perfect this dish with its slightly sweet and crispy crust and flavorful delicate chicken filling.

Serves 6 to 8

¼ cup vegetable oil
½ cup yellow onion, diced
4 cloves of garlic, finely minced
½ cup red bell pepper or a combination of red and green
1 teaspoon garlic powder
1 teaspoon onion powder
½ teaspoon ground cumin
½ teaspoon dried oregano
1½ teaspoons salt or more, to taste
1½ to 2 pounds boneless, skinless chicken fillets or breast, coarsely chopped
¾ cup crushed tomatoes
¼ cup *vino seco* (dry white cooking wine)
¼ cup raisins
¼ cup chopped green olives
nonstick cooking spray
2 refrigerated pie crusts
1 egg beaten with a tablespoon of water (optional: add 2 teaspoons sugar for added sweetness)

◈ In a large covered skillet over medium heat, heat ¼ cup oil, add onions, garlic, and bell peppers, and cook for 5 to 7 minutes or until the onion is slightly translucent. Add all the spices and about half the salt and continue cooking.

Add the chicken and continue cooking for about 8 minutes, stirring occasionally.

Add tomatoes, wine, raisins, olives, and remaining salt and reduce heat to low and cover. Continue cooking for 1½ hours. Remove from heat and set aside to cool.

Preheat oven to 400°F. Spray a large pie plate with nonstick spray. Place one of the refrigerated pie disks in the pie plate and mold lightly to the plate, removing any of the dough that hangs over; do not discard remaining dough in case you want to use it to decorate the edges. Poke some holes in the dough with the tines of a fork and place in the oven for 5 minutes. Remove from oven and allow to cool (this may be done in advance). Reduce temperature to 350°F.

Fill the pie shell with the chicken mixture and top with the other pie disk. Fold the edges over and into the pie pan. You may decorate with a scalloped edge or use a fork to seal. Place a slit or two in the center to allow steam to escape. Brush the top with the egg wash. Place in the 350° oven for 20 to 25 minutes or until golden brown. May be served hot or at room temperature.

Note: This recipe is a little different from Versailles' Pastelón de Pollo Santiaguero in that it uses refrigerated pie crust. The pastry made at the bakery is too labor intensive to include here. Mix the sugar into the egg wash for the top of the crust before baking if you want that little extra sweetness.

You don't
NO QUIERES
want soup
CALDO PERO COGES
but you take
TRES TAZAS.
three bowls.

SOUPS AND STEWS

Nothing satisfies like a bowl of soup or a rich, hearty stew. Soups and stews have become the cornerstone of Cuban cuisine. Growing up, it was the mainstay of our diets—it was rare to have a meal that did not include beans or soup as a starter, for it was part of the Cuban mother's and grandmother's quest to put some meat on our bones. Grandmothers always say, "*Tómate una sopita*" (have a little soup). There is a mentality among Cuban moms and grandmas that soup will cure everything from the common cold to a broken heart. We're not saying any of these soups will cure what ails you, but you will certainly feel happy and satisfied after indulging in a hot bowl of nutritious and tasty goodness.

Soups are popular at Cuban restaurants and an integral part of Cuban cuisine in general. Many are much closer to a stew, laden with meats and vegetables. This chapter contains a good variety and our most popular—everything from basic Cuban-style chicken soup (Cuban penicillin) to the hearty, Spanish-influenced Caldo Gallego. Cook up a batch of one of these when the season is getting a little cool or you are feeling a bit under the weather. Our grandmas promise a quick and full recovery.

Black Bean Soup ◈ Frijoles Negros

Every Cuban cookbook offers a recipe for black bean soup. No dish says "Cuban" more than black beans, and ours are by far the best! You'll be hard-pressed to find a plate that comes out of our kitchen that is not ordered with a side of these deliciously decadent black beans. Soaking your beans the night before you cook them makes the cooking process much quicker and produces beans that are uniformly tender.

Serves 6 to 8

1 pound dry black beans, picked
   through and rinsed
¼ cup olive oil
1 large onion, chopped
3 garlic cloves, minced
1 green bell pepper, chopped
1 bay leaf
½ teaspoon ground cumin
2 tablespoons white wine vinegar
2 tablespoons sugar
salt and pepper
cooked white rice

◈ Place the beans in a large bowl and add enough room temperature water to cover. Soak the beans for at least 6 hours, preferably overnight. (If you are soaking them for 6 hours, use slightly warm or tepid water instead.)

Drain the beans and set them aside. Heat the olive oil in a large stockpot over medium heat. Add the onion, garlic, and bell pepper and sauté for 5 to 7 minutes, until the vegetables soften.

Add the bay leaf and cumin and stir well. Add the beans and 1½ quarts water and bring to a boil. Let the soup boil for about 10 minutes, then reduce the heat to low. Add the vinegar and sugar and stir well. Cover the pot and let the soup simmer for 3 to 3½ hours, until the beans are soft and tender and the stock has thickened. (The stock will continue to thicken as the beans cool to room temperature.) Remove and discard the bay leaf. Season the soup generously with salt and a sprinkling of pepper. Serve over long grain white rice.

Cream of Malanga ◈ Crema de Malanga

Malanga is a taro-like root vegetable to most, but to Cubans it is a cure-all. Whether you have a cold or a toothache, just had a baby or took a big exam, this creamy soup will cure what ails you.

Serves 6 to 8

2½ pounds malanga, peeled and cut into chunks

4 cups water

2 garlic cloves, minced and sautéed in a little butter or margarine

½ cup heavy cream or half and half

2 tablespoons butter or margarine

1 teaspoon salt

◈ In a deep pot, cook malanga with water for about 35–40 minutes, or until tender. Remove malanga and drain all but ½ cup of the cooking liquid. Put malanga into a blender, add sautéed garlic, and purée. Strain using a sieve. Return to blender and add remaining ingredients, including enough of the cooking liquid to attain desired consistency, and blend until creamy. Add more salt if necessary. Top with malanga chips and serve immediately.

Galician White Bean Soup ◈ Caldo Gallego

This soup originated in Galicia, Spain, and is very popular in Cuban kitchens—including ours. It is a robust and nutritious dish perfect on a cold night with some crusty bread and a hearty Spanish wine.

Serves 8 to 10

1 pound dry white beans (such as navy, cannellini, or great northern), rinsed, soaked overnight, and drained
½ pound ham hock or shank bones
3 ounces cured pork fatback or salt pork, rind removed
½ pound pork belly or pancetta, diced and sautéed until golden brown
1 large onion, diced
3 garlic cloves, minced
3 medium potatoes, diced
1 small turnip, diced
salt and white pepper to taste
2 cups chopped fresh collard greens or turnip greens
3 tablespoons olive oil

◈ Combine 2 quarts water, beans, ham hock, pork fatback, pork belly, onion, and garlic in a large pot over medium-high heat. Bring the soup to a boil; boil for 10 minutes. Reduce the heat to low, cover the pot, and cook the soup for 2 to 2½ hours.

Remove the soup from the heat and let it sit for 15 to 30 minutes, so that the soup can thicken and the flavors come together. Remove the ham hock and fatback from the pot, discarding the fatback. Remove the meat from the ham hock and return it to the soup. Discard the bones.

Add the potatoes, turnip, and salt and pepper to taste. Cover the pot and let the soup cook over low heat for another 30 to 45 minutes, until the potatoes are fork-tender. During the last 10 minutes of the cooking process, add the collard greens and olive oil. Taste the soup and adjust the seasonings, if necessary.

Nadie escarmienta por cabeza agena.

Nobody learns from someone else's mistake.

Red Bean Soup ◈ Frijoles Colorados

Another favorite in Cuban cuisine, red bean soup is quite different from the ever-popular black bean soup. The Santiagueros grew up on this stuff, for as popular as black beans were in Cuba, red beans were so in Santiago. Here the tomato base and chorizo impart a tangy and unique flavor to the beans. The addition of vegetables makes this a perfect one-dish meal: nutritious and savory.

Tip: Make sure you don't confuse these small, oval, red beans with kidney beans.

Serves 6 to 8

1 pound dry red beans

¼ cup olive oil

1 large onion, diced

3 garlic cloves, minced

1 medium green bell pepper, chopped

1 cup crushed tomatoes

1 cup *vino seco* (dry white cooking wine)

¼ pound ham hock, optional

½ pound Spanish chorizo sausage

1 bay leaf

1 teaspoon sweet paprika

½ teaspoon cumin

1 cup peeled and diced red-skinned
  potatoes

1 cup ripe diced plantains

1 cup chopped calabaza (Cuban squash)

salt and pepper

Mas sabe el diablo por viejo que por diablo.

The devil knows more from old age than from being the devil.

◈ Place the beans in a large bowl and add enough room temperature water to cover. Soak the beans for at least 6 hours, preferably overnight. (If you are soaking them for 6 hours, use slightly warm or tepid water instead.)

Drain the beans and set them aside. Heat the olive oil in a skillet or sauté pan over medium heat. Add the onion, garlic, and bell pepper and sauté for 5 to 7 minutes, until the vegetables soften. Add crushed tomato and cook for an additional 5 minutes. Set aside.

In a large stockpot combine 1½ quarts of water, *vino seco*, ham hock, chorizo, and bay leaf and raise the heat to medium-high. Bring the soup to a boil, stirring frequently. Let the soup boil for 20 minutes. Add the beans, reduce the heat to low, cover the pot, and cook the soup for 1 hour; then add the tomato-based *sofrito* and cook another 1 to 1½ hours, until it thickens slightly and the beans are tender. Remove the bay leaf, chorizo, and ham hock. Cut the chorizo into ½-inch slices and return them to the pot. Discard the bay leaf and ham hock. Add the remaining dry spices.

Add the potatoes and plantains and cook for 15 minutes, then add the calabaza and bring the soup to a boil. Reduce the heat to low and cover. Continue cooking over low heat until the vegetables are fork-tender. Add more salt and pepper to taste, if necessary. This soup may be served alone or over fluffy white rice.

Chickpea Soup ◆ Potaje de Garbanzos

This soup is quite hearty and nutritious. It can easily be served as a main course with some white rice.

Serves 8 to 10

1 pound dried chickpeas, rinsed, soaked overnight, and drained

½ pound ham hock

1 bay leaf

¼ cup olive oil, plus more as needed

1 cup diced onion

½ cup diced green bell pepper

4 garlic cloves, minced

1½ cups crushed tomatoes

3 medium white potatoes, peeled and cubed

2 cups cubed calabaza (Cuban squash)

¾ pound Spanish chorizo sausage, sliced

¼ pound pork belly or pancetta, diced and sautéed until golden brown

½ ham steak cut in ½-inch cubes

1 tablespoon sweet paprika

½ teaspoon cumin

salt

½ teaspoon white pepper

Ni comes ni dejas de comer.

You don't eat but you don't let anybody eat either.

◆ Fill a large pot three-quarters full with water and bring it to a boil. Add the chickpeas, ham hock, and bay leaf. Reduce the heat to low and cook the soup, covered, for 3 to 3½ hours, until the chickpeas are tender. You may need to add more water during the cooking process—the pot should always be about three-quarters full.

Heat the olive oil in a pan over medium heat. Add the onion, bell pepper, and garlic and sauté for 5 to 7 minutes, until the onion is translucent. Add the crushed tomatoes and cook for another 5 minutes.

Add the tomato mixture to the soup, followed by the potatoes, calabaza, chorizo, pork belly, ham, paprika, cumin, and salt and pepper to taste. Bring the soup to a boil, stirring frequently, and let boil for 3 minutes. Reduce the heat to low, cover the pot, and let the soup simmer for another 30 minutes. Adjust the seasonings, if necessary. Remove and discard the bay leaf. Serve with a drizzle of olive oil and a side of steaming white rice.

Tip: In a pinch you may use crumbled bacon to replace the pork belly or pancetta, which will give the finished dish a slightly smokier flavor.

Asturian Bean Stew ◆ Fabada Asturiana

Cubans love Fabada, a rich bean stew that is a close cousin to the classic French cassoulet and originated in Asturias, Spain. Some of the ingredients in this stew are unique and may be difficult to find. You may substitute cannellini beans for *fabas* with excellent results.

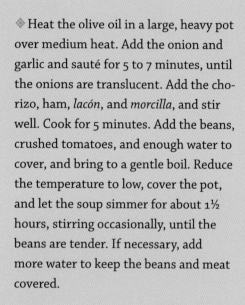

Serves 6

¼ cup extra virgin olive oil

1 small white onion, finely sliced

2 garlic cloves, minced

¾ pound Spanish chorizo sausage

½ pound ham steak or cooking ham, cubed

¾ pound *lacón* (smoked pork shank) or ham hocks, optional

½ pound *morcilla* (blood sausage), optional

1 pound *fabas*, cannellini, or other white beans, rinsed, soaked overnight, and drained

1 cup crushed tomatoes

1 teaspoon sweet paprika

½ teaspoon ground cumin

3 or 4 saffron threads

½ teaspoon white pepper

salt

parsley

◆ Heat the olive oil in a large, heavy pot over medium heat. Add the onion and garlic and sauté for 5 to 7 minutes, until the onions are translucent. Add the chorizo, ham, *lacón*, and *morcilla*, and stir well. Cook for 5 minutes. Add the beans, crushed tomatoes, and enough water to cover, and bring to a gentle boil. Reduce the temperature to low, cover the pot, and let the soup simmer for about 1½ hours, stirring occasionally, until the beans are tender. If necessary, add more water to keep the beans and meat covered.

Remove the soup from the heat, add spices, and cool to room temperature to allow the flavors and textures of the soup to develop. Taste the soup and add salt to taste.

If necessary, reheat the soup before serving. Garnish with parsley and a drizzle of olive oil.

No hay mal que por bien no venga.

Something good comes out of a bad experience.

Tropical Soup ◈ Ajiaco

This is the "kitchen sink stew," and once you look at the number of ingredients in this recipe, you'll know why. Some people say that Ajiaco is Cuba's national dish, and while we have not been able to confirm that, we can confirm that it is very popular at Versailles.

Serves 8 to 10

½ pound *tasajo* (salt-cured beef)

1 quart low-sodium chicken stock

2 pounds pork loin, cut into 1-inch chunks

1 bay leaf

1 malanga, peeled and cut into 1½-inch cubes

1 yuca, cut into 1½-inch cubes

1 boniato, peeled and cut into 1½-inch cubes

1 green plantain, peeled and cut into 2-inch-thick slices

3 ears corn, cut into 2-inch-thick slices

1¾-pound calabaza, peeled and cut into 1½-inch cubes

1 sweet (black) plantain, peeled and cut into 1-inch-thick slices

½ cup olive oil

4 garlic cloves, chopped

1 medium green bell pepper, chopped

2 medium onions, chopped

1 cup crushed tomatoes

½ teaspoon dried oregano

½ teaspoon ground cumin

1 teaspoon sweet paprika

1 to 2 teaspoons salt

½ teaspoon white pepper

◆ Place the *tasajo* in a bowl and add lukewarm water to cover. Soak overnight. Rinse, drain, and set aside.

Bring 2 quarts water and 1 quart chicken stock to a boil in a large stockpot over high heat. Add the *tasajo*, pork, and bay leaf. Reduce the heat to medium-low and simmer for 1½ hours—the broth should reduce by about one-third. Skim the top of the stock occasionally to remove any residue.

Add the malanga, yuca, boniato, green plantain, and corn. Stir, cover, and cook for 15 to 20 minutes. Add remaining vegetables, stir, cover, and continue cooking for 15 mintes or until all vegetables are fork tender. (You may need to add additional liquid to keep the vegetables covered.)

Heat the olive oil in a pan over medium-high heat. Add the garlic, bell pepper, and onion, and sauté for 5 to 7 minutes, until the vegetables soften and the flavors are well incorporated. Add the crushed tomato and lower the heat. Simmer for 20 minutes.

Add the tomato mixture to the stockpot and stir well. Stir in the oregano, cumin, paprika, salt, and pepper. Remove and discard the bay leaf.

Tip: It is not necessary to make stock from scratch for many of these soups and stews. There are some great top quality boxed stocks available at most markets. Just taste before adding salt, as many of them contain quite a bit of sodium already.

A mal tiempo, buena cara.

Chin up during difficult times.

Chicken Soup ◈ Sopa de Pollo

We like to call this Cuban penicillin. It is certainly popular at the restaurant when cold and 'flu season hits. But don't wait to be sick to enjoy this delicious and nutritious soup—it's wonderful at any season, warm enough for the winter and light enough for the summer. It is a cultural staple! Cubans brag about who makes the best chicken soup in town, and Versailles is definitely high on the list.

Serves 6 to 8

2 quarts low-sodium chicken stock
1 whole chicken or 4 chicken breast
   halves, bone in, skin removed
1 garlic clove
1 bay leaf
1 carrot, diced
2 celery stalks, diced
1 large ripe tomato, seeded
1 medium onion, diced
1 teaspoon salt, plus more as needed
½ teaspoon bijol (yellow coloring)
4 ounces *fideos* or angel hair pasta
white pepper (optional)
lime wedge, for serving

◈ Bring 2 quarts of chicken stock to a boil in a large pot. Add the chicken breasts, garlic, bay leaf, carrot, celery, tomato, onion, and salt. Reduce the heat to low, cover the pot, and simmer for at least 1 hour, until the chicken is cooked through and opaque.

Transfer the chicken to a plate and set aside. Discard all the vegetables, the garlic, and bay leaf. Transfer the stock to another container and allow it to cool completely. Place in refrigerator for an hour and remove the solidified fat layer on top.

Heat the chicken stock in the stockpot. Add the bijol and stir well. Remove the chicken from the bone and tear it into pieces with your hands. (We prefer this method to chopping it with a knife because the chicken retains more moisture and flavor.) Add the chicken and the *fideos* to the hot stock and stir to incorporate. Bring the soup to a boil again, then immediately turn off the heat and season the soup with salt and pepper to taste. Stir well and add a squeeze of lime before serving.

El mono aunque se vista de seda, mono se queda.

A monkey dressed in silk is still a monkey.

Split Pea Soup ◈ Chícharos

This split pea soup is comfort food in the truest sense of the word. It is rich and creamy and very satisfying.

Serves 6 to 8

½ pound Spanish chorizo sausage, sliced

1 ham hock

1 bay leaf

1 pound peeled *chícharos* (split peas)

¼ cup olive oil, plus more as needed

2 garlic cloves, minced

1 medium onion, chopped

1 small green bell pepper, chopped

½ cup crushed tomatoes

4 medium potatoes, cut into 1-inch chunks

1 cup chopped calabaza

1 teaspoon sweet paprika

½ teaspoon ground cumin

1 teaspoon salt

½ teaspoon white pepper

◈ Bring 3 quarts of water to a boil in a large stockpot. Add the chorizo, ham hock, and bay leaf and reduce the heat to low. Let the soup simmer for about 15 minutes. Add the split peas and cook an additional 35 minutes.

Meanwhile, heat the oil in a large frying pan over medium-high heat. Add the garlic, onion, and bell pepper and lightly sauté for 5 to 7 minutes, until soft, then add the crushed tomato and cook for another 5 minutes. Set aside.

After the peas have simmered for 35 minutes, add the tomato/*sofrito* mixture, the potatoes, calabaza, paprika, cumin, salt, and pepper to the stockpot. Cook for another 30 minutes, stirring frequently.

Remove the soup from the heat and let it cool to room temperature, to allow the soup to thicken and the flavors to come together completely. Remove and discard the bay leaf. Taste the soup and adjust the seasonings, if necessary. Reheat the soup to the desired temperature and serve with a drizzle of olive oil on top.

Dime con quien andas y te diré quien eres.

Tell me who your friends are, and I'll tell you who you are.

Hearty Lentil Soup ◈ Potaje de Lentejas

Lentil soup is a Cuban favorite because it is so hearty and nutritious. Each Cuban restaurant has its own version. Versailles' lentil soup is chock full of meat and veggies and, we think you will agree, the best anywhere.

Serves 6 to 8

¼ cup olive oil

¼ pound cooking ham, diced

¼ pound Spanish chorizo sausage, diced

3 garlic cloves, minced

½ cup diced green bell pepper

1 large onion, diced

6 cups homemade or low-sodium canned chicken stock

½ cup crushed tomatoes

1 pound dried lentils, rinsed in cold water and soaked for 30 minutes

2 large white potatoes, peeled and cut into 1-inch pieces

3 carrots, peeled and diced into ½-inch pieces

1 bay leaf

½ teaspoon ground cumin

½ teaspoon sweet paprika

½ teaspoon salt

½ teaspoon white pepper

◈ Heat half the olive oil in a large stockpot over medium heat. Add the ham and chorizo and sauté for 3 to 5 minutes, until the chorizo browns slightly. Add the garlic, bell pepper, and onion and cook for another 5 minutes, until the onion softens.

Add the remaining ingredients and stir well. Bring the soup to a boil over medium heat and continue boiling for 5 minutes. Reduce the heat to low, cover the pot, and continue cooking, stirring occasionally, for 45 minutes to 1 hour, until the vegetables and lentils are tender. Taste and adjust the seasonings as necessary. Remove and discard the bay leaf.

Ponte pa tu número.

Get on your number.*

*Get it together.

Cuban-Style Fish Stew ◈ Sopa de Pescado

Similar to *cioppino*, the fish soup created by Italian immigrant fishermen in San Francisco, Sopa de Pescado makes a wonderful lunch or light dinner. It's delicious with some crusty bread; the patrons at Versailles usually order an extra basket of bread with this soup.

Serves 6 to 8

¼ cup olive oil, plus more as needed
3 garlic cloves, minced
1 large onion, diced
½ cup diced carrots
3 tablespoons crushed tomatoes
1 teaspoon sweet paprika
1 bay leaf
½ teaspoon bijol (yellow coloring)
1 teaspoon garlic powder
6 cups low-sodium fish stock
1 cup diced white potato
2 pounds mahimahi or any other firm white fish cut into 2-inch chunks
salt and pepper, to taste
2 cups cooked long grain white rice
¼ cup finely chopped flat leaf parsley
lime wedges, for garnish

◈ Heat the olive oil in a large, heavy pot over medium heat. Add the garlic and onion and sauté for 5 to 7 minutes, until the vegetables soften. Add the carrots and cook an additional 5 minutes. Add the crushed tomato, paprika, bay leaf, bijol, garlic powder, and stock and bring to a boil. Add the potatoes; reduce the heat to low, and cover the pot. Cook for 20 to 30 minutes, until the potatoes are soft.

Add the fish to the soup and stir lightly. The fish will cook in about 5 minutes; you'll know it's cooked when it is opaque in the center. Taste the soup and adjust the seasonings, if necessary. Add the cooked rice and stir well.

Garnish the soup with parsley and serve with lime wedges and a drizzle of olive oil.

Le cayó comején al piano.

The piano got termites.*

* Things just got ugly.

Plantain Soup ◆ Sopa de Plátano

This rich and delectable plantain soup is representative of our Cuban flavors—savory with a touch of sweetness. Make some plantain chips to go along with it and you will not be disappointed.

Serves 6

oil for frying
3 green plantains, peeled and sliced into
   1½-inch slices
2 tablespoons olive oil
3 cloves garlic, finely minced
3 cups low-sodium chicken stock
3 cups low-sodium beef stock
1 teaspoon salt
½ teaspoon ground cumin
½ teaspoon white pepper
½ teaspoon bijol (yellow coloring)
Mariquitas (Plantain Chips) for garnish

◆ In a large skillet heat about 2 inches of oil over medium heat. Fry the plantain slices for about 3 minutes per side; do not allow them to brown. Drain the plantains on a paper towel–lined platter. Fry ⅓ of the plantains again for 3 minutes per side over medium heat. Set them aside.

Heat the olive oil in a large, heavy pot over medium heat. Add the garlic and sauté for 5 minutes. Combine all the rest of the ingredients except ⅓ of the plantains in a large stockpot and cook over high heat until boiling rapidly. Boil for 3 minutes, stirring frequently.

Reduce the heat to low, cover the pot, and simmer for 35 to 40 minutes, until the plantains are tender. Add the reserved twice fried plantains to the stockpot halfway through the cooking process (after about 20 minutes). Remove the pot from the heat and allow the soup to cool a bit.

Using an immersion blender or working carefully in very small batches with a standard blender or food processor, purée the soup until it is creamy. Taste the soup and adjust the seasonings, if necessary. Serve hot, garnished with Mariquitas (Plantain Chips—see recipe, page 24).

Soft Polenta with Pork ◈ Tamal en Cazuela

Tamal en Cazuela is basically a creamy version of tamales. Similar to, but heartier than, polenta, the addition of pork makes it very Cuban.

Serves 6 to 8

1 pound lean pork loin, cut into 1-inch
    chunks
salt and pepper
⅓ cup olive oil
1 large onion, chopped
4 garlic cloves, minced
1½ cups crushed tomatoes
½ teaspoon ground cumin
1 cup whole milk
½ teaspoon bijol (yellow coloring)
2 teaspoons salt
½ teaspoon white pepper
1½ cups yellow cornmeal
1 cup corn off the husk, finely chopped
    or pulsed in a food processor
salt and white pepper to taste

◈ Season pork generously with salt and pepper and set aside.

Heat 2 tablespoons of the olive oil in a sauté pan over medium heat. Add the onion and garlic and sauté for 5 to 7 minutes, until the vegetables soften. Add the crushed tomato and cumin and bring to a boil. Reduce heat, cover the pan, and simmer for 15 to 20 minutes, allowing the sauce to cook down a bit. Set aside.

In a separate frying pan, heat 2 to 3 tablespoons of the olive oil (depending on how lean your meat is) over medium-high heat. Add the pork and sear the pieces on all sides. Reduce the heat to medium and cook for another 5 minutes. Set aside.

In a large stockpot, bring 1½ quarts water, milk, and bijol to a boil. Add 2 teaspoons salt, ½ teaspoon pepper, and the remaining olive oil. Add the cornmeal while stirring continuously with a wire whisk. Reduce the heat to low and continue cooking, stirring occasionally, for 30 to 45 minutes, until the mixture thickens and becomes creamy. Add the corn and stir well. Taste and adjust the seasonings, if necessary.

To serve, add the crispy pork chunks atop or mixed into a steaming bowl of this dense, creamy soup. Season with hot sauce and a squeeze of lime if desired.

That
ESE HUEVO
egg wants
QUIERE SAL.
salt.*

*Someone is looking for a good time.

eGG DISHeS AND SALADS

Yes, salads—Cubans do eat them. No, they are not complex salads with blackened shrimp or grilled chicken breast on top of fifteen ingredients. They are simple add-ons to our already rich and flavorful main courses.

This section is short but important because the dishes are so popular. An avocado salad is a must before a good Arroz con Pollo. The creamy Chicken Salad always accompanies the delicious croquettes. Our recent addition, the Versailles Salad, makes a great light meal. And the big-enough-to-share omelets are a late night favorite at our restaurant.

Avocado Salad ◈ Ensalada de Aguacate

This salad is just the right prelude to many Cuban dishes. The creaminess of a perfectly ripe avocado and the tangy vinaigrette complement our savory dishes perfectly. Don't cut the avocado too long before serving this salad, as it will oxidize and turn brown quickly. But if you need to cut it ahead of time, squeeze some lime juice over it.

Serves 4

¼ cup red wine vinegar
½ teaspoon salt
¼ teaspoon white pepper
¼ cup olive oil
1 large ripe avocado or 2 small ones, cut into thick slices
1 medium red onion, very thinly sliced

◈ Whisk together the vinegar, salt, and white pepper in a bowl. Continue whisking as you add the olive oil in a slow, steady stream.

Arrange the avocado on a platter, then top with slices of onion. Pour the dressing over the salad and serve immediately.

Chicken Salad ◈ Ensalada de Pollo

The Chicken Salad is a best seller at Versailles. It is served with 2 freshly fried ham croquettes and saltine crackers. It is a little labor intensive compared to your average salad, but the reward is worth the effort, and it will keep several days in the refrigerator.

Serves 6 to 8

4 large red potatoes, peeled and cut into 1-inch cubes

1 cup mayonnaise, plus more as needed

1 tablespoon yellow mustard

2 tablespoons diced pimientos

1 teaspoon garlic powder

1 teaspoon onion powder

salt to taste

½ teaspoon white pepper

1 whole roasted chicken, skinned, deboned, and hand shredded (you may also use all white meat)

1 large red delicious apple, peeled, cored, and cut into ½-inch cubes

3 hard-boiled eggs, chopped

◈ Place the potatoes in a pot with just enough salted water to cover them, and bring to a boil. Continue boiling, uncovered, for 15 to 20 minutes, until the potatoes are fork-tender. Drain and set aside.

In a large bowl, whisk together the mayonnaise, mustard, pimientos, garlic powder, onion powder, and salt and pepper to taste. Add the chicken and stir well. Taste the salad and adjust the seasonings, if necessary. Add the apple and eggs and toss the salad with your hands to prevent the eggs and soft vegetables from breaking apart. If the salad looks too dry, add a couple more tablespoons of mayonnaise.

Tip: You may wish to decorate the bowl in which you serve the salad by lining it with romaine lettuce leaves and topping it with additional sliced hard-boiled egg, peas, and pimientos.

Si mi abuela tuviera ruedas, fuera bicicleta.

If my grandmother had wheels, she'd be a bicycle.

Versailles Salad

While not traditionally Cuban, the Versailles Salad is becoming increasingly popular at the restaurant. The combination of mango and goat cheese is unexpected and delicious.

Makes 1 large salad

2 cups of spring mix lettuce
2 ounces Honey Balsamic Vinaigrette
⅛ cup julienned red onion
½ cup diced mango
3 tablespoons candied pecans
1 ounce goat cheese (crumbled)

◈ In a salad bowl combine the spring mix, honey balsamic vinaigrette, and red onion and place on a large plate. Place the remaining ingredients (mango, pecans, and cheese) on top of the salad making three small mounds, with the goat cheese in the center. Serve immediately.

Honey Balsamic Vinaigrette

¼ cup balsamic vinegar
2 tablespoons honey
½ cup olive oil
salt and ground black pepper to taste

Whisk ingredients together in a small bowl. This will make more dressing than you need. The rest will keep in a covered container for a week.

Le ronca el mango.
The mango snores.*

*Too much to handle or simply ridiculous.

Potato Omelet ◆ Tortilla de Papas

You would think omelets would be more popular as a breakfast item, but the late night crowd really loves the variety of omelets available at Versailles. This simple yet satisfying potato omelet is a Cuban classic.

Serves 2 to 4

2 to 3 cups vegetable oil
2 large potatoes, peeled and cut into
 ½-inch cubes
¼ cup olive oil
6 large eggs
1 teaspoon salt
½ teaspoon pepper
1 tablespoon baby peas
1 tablespoon pimientos

◆ Heat about 2 inches of vegetable oil in a large frying pan over medium-high heat. Carefully place the potatoes in the oil in a single layer and reduce heat to medium. Fry the potatoes for 5 to 7 minutes, until they are a light golden brown. Transfer the cooked potatoes to a paper towel to drain and cool to room temperature. (You can also use leftover potatoes in this; just be sure they are at room temperature before adding them to the omelet.)

Heat the olive oil in a medium nonstick frying pan over medium heat. Add the potatoes and spread them out evenly, so they cover the bottom of the pan and are evenly distributed.

Crack the eggs into a large bowl, add the salt and pepper, and mix thoroughly with a fork. Pour the eggs evenly over the potato. Allow the omelet to cook, undisturbed, for 5 to 7 minutes, until the bottom of the omelet is golden brown and set.

Slide the omelet carefully onto a plate (preferably one that is larger than the pan), flip the pan over the plate, then quickly invert them both, so that the uncooked side of the omelet ends up face-down in the pan. Cook for 4 to 5 minutes. Slide the omelet onto a plate, cut it into wedges, and serve immediately, garnished with peas and pimientos.

Note: If inverting the plate seems too complicated, place the frying pan under a hot broiler for a few minutes (watch it closely). You can even leave the oven door open, with the handle of the pan sticking out. This method works just as well, with no egg acrobatics!

Sweet Plantain Omelet ◈ Tortilla de Platanitos Maduros

This particular omelet is best as a dinner or a late night meal with a side of white rice, and while the combination may sound a little odd, it is surprisingly tasty. This recipe provides instructions for freshly fried plantains, but feel free to use plantains that were previously fried. Just warm them for a few minutes in the pan before adding the eggs. Your plantains should be ripe for this recipe, soft to the touch, with black skins.

Serves 2 to 4

2 to 3 cups olive oil, plus more as needed
2 very ripe (black) plantains, peeled and cut diagonally into ½-inch slices
6 large eggs
1 teaspoon salt
½ teaspoon pepper
1 tablespoon peas
1 tablespoon pimientos

◈ Heat about 3 inches of oil to about 375°F in a heavy pot. Add 4 or 5 plantain slices to the hot oil and cook for about 3 minutes on each side, turning only once, until the plantains are golden brown. Using a slotted spoon, transfer the fried plantains to a paper towel to drain. Continue with the remaining plantain slices.

Heat 2 tablespoons olive oil in a medium nonstick frying pan over medium heat. Space the fried plantains evenly on the bottom of the pan.

Crack the eggs into a large bowl, add the salt and pepper, and mix thoroughly with a fork. Pour the eggs evenly into the pan over the plantains. Allow the omelet to cook, undisturbed, for 5 to 7 minutes, until the bottom of the omelet is golden brown and set.

Slide the omelet carefully onto a plate (preferably one that is larger than the pan), flip the pan over the plate, then quickly invert them both, so that the uncooked side of the omelet ends up face-down in the pan. Cook for 4 to 5 minutes. Slide the omelet onto a plate, cut it into wedges, and serve immediately, garnished with peas and pimientos.

Basque Omelet ◈ Tortilla Vasca

Spain's influence on Cuban food is pretty extensive. This *tortilla* is a great example. It can be served hot or at room temperature. Brimming with potatoes, chorizo, and onions, it's a meal in itself.

Serves 2 to 4

3 tablespoons olive oil

¼ cup cooked ham, diced

½ pound Spanish chorizo sausage,
   roughly chopped

¼ pound peeled and deveined medium
   shrimp, cut in half (tail off)

6 large eggs

1 teaspoon salt

½ teaspoon pepper

1 tablespoon baby peas

1 tablespoon pimientos

◈ Heat the olive oil in a medium nonstick frying pan over medium heat. Add the chorizo and ham and sauté for 2 to 3 minutes. Add the shrimp and cook an additional 3 minutes or until opaque. Spread them out evenly, so they cover the bottom of the pan and are evenly distributed among the rest of the ingredients.

Crack the eggs into a large bowl, add the salt and pepper, and mix thoroughly with a fork. Pour the eggs evenly over the shrimp-chorizo-ham mixture. Allow the omelet to cook, undisturbed, for 5 to 7 minutes, until the bottom of the omelet is golden brown and set.

Slide the omelet carefully onto a plate (preferably one that is larger than the pan), flip the pan over the plate, then quickly invert them both, so that the uncooked side of the omelet ends up face-down in the pan. Cook for 4 to 5 minutes. Slide the omelet onto a plate, cut it into wedges, and serve immediately, garnished with peas and pimientos.

Don't take NO LLEVES sand to the ARENA A LA beach.* PLAYA.

*Don't state the obvious.

FISH AND SEAFOOD

You shouldn't be surprised that there are numerous dishes at Versailles that include fish and shellfish. After all, Cuba is an island—and, if you recall, the setting for Ernest Hemingway's *The Old Man and the Sea*.

Even though our culinary heritage has the bad reputation of wreaking havoc on our waistlines, there are a few recipes in this chapter that could be deemed light and even figure friendly. Because Cuba is surrounded by water, fish is plentiful. Traditional Cuban fish recipes are delicious and quite simple. A whole fried snapper with little more than a squeeze of lime is one of our staples. However, Spain's influences on our fish and shellfish recipes provide some very exciting options. This chapter is a wonderful example of how to make the most of the sea's bounty.

Fish in Parsley and Garlic Sauce ◈ Pescado en Salsa Verde

There are many variations to the preparation of this dish, which is originally from Spain. While the recipe calls for snapper, almost any white flaky fish will work. We recommend hand chopping the parsley instead of using a food processor, so as to retain the vibrant green color.

Serves 6

3 tablespoons salted butter
½ cup olive oil, plus more as needed
8 garlic cloves, minced
½ cup diced sweet onion (like Vidalia)
½ cup *vino seco* (dry white cooking wine)
¼ cup clam juice
juice of 1 lime
1 teaspoon salt
½ teaspoon white pepper
1½ cups chopped parsley
6 (6- to 8-ounce) fresh cod fillets, or other firm-fleshed white fish
all-purpose flour for dredging fish
3 sliced hard-boiled eggs
2 tablespoons baby peas
pimientos

◈ Heat butter and half the olive oil in a large sauté pan over medium heat. Sauté garlic and onion 3 to 4 minutes, until translucent. Add the wine, clam juice, and lime and cook an additional 5 to 7 minutes. Add ½ teaspoon of salt and white pepper. Taste and add more salt if necessary. Add parsley and cook 2 minutes more. Set aside.

In a separate pan heat the remaining olive oil. Season the fish fillets generously with salt and white pepper, dredge lightly in flour, and cook approximately 3 minutes per side, until opaque. Remove the fish from the pan and add it to the pan with the sauce. Cook an additional minute to heat through. Serve with sauce spooned over and garnished with hard-boiled egg, peas, and pimientos.

Shrimp in Garlic Sauce ◆ Camarones al Ajillo

This garlic-based dish is favored among our patrons as a nice change of pace from the ever-popular Camarones Enchilados (see next recipe).

Serves 6 to 8

2 pounds medium shrimp, peeled and
   deveined, tails on
all-purpose flour for dredging
4 tablespoons salted butter
¾ cup olive oil
15 garlic cloves, minced
¼ cup *vino seco* (dry white cooking wine)
¼ cup clam juice
juice of 1 lime
2 teaspoons salt, plus more for
   seasoning shrimp
½ teaspoon white pepper, plus more for
   seasoning shrimp
¼ cup diced parsley
cooked white rice

◆ Season shrimp with salt and white pepper; dredge lightly in flour and set aside. In a heavy pot, heat 2 tablespoons of the butter over medium heat. Once the butter begins to turn golden brown, add half of the shrimp and quickly sear them (you may have to raise the heat). Transfer the shrimp to a plate and repeat with the remaining butter and shrimp.

In the same pot, heat the olive oil over medium heat. Add the garlic and sauté for 2 to 3 minutes, until soft. Add the wine, clam juice, lime juice, salt, and pepper, and bring to a boil. Reduce the heat to low, cover the pot, and cook for 15 to 20 minutes. You may need to add extra clam juice if the sauce evaporates too quickly, but not more than ¼ cup. Cook for 5 to 7 minutes, add the shrimp to heat through, and serve with white rice.

Tip: Shrimp cook very quickly, usually in a minute or two. Cook only until opaque, as the residual heat continues to cook them. Never overcook shrimp, or they will be tough.

Shrimp Creole ◆ Camarones Enchilados

This popular and traditional shrimp dish is made special at Versailles by its slow simmer process in the Versailles *sofrito*. Because shrimp is delicately flavored, the *sofrito* sauce really highlights this dish. It is equally delicious with lobster.

Serves 6

⅓ cup olive oil

4 garlic cloves, minced

1 large onion, diced

½ cup green bell pepper, diced

½ cup red bell pepper, diced

1¼ cups crushed tomatoes

¼ cup ketchup

¼ cup *vino seco* (dry white cooking wine)

¼ cup clam juice

1 bay leaf

1 teaspoon salt

1 teaspoon pepper

1 teaspoon sweet paprika

½ teaspoon dried oregano

2 pounds medium shrimp, peeled and deveined

1 tablespoon baby peas

1 tablespoon chopped parsley

◈ Heat the olive oil in a large, heavy pot over medium-high heat. Add the garlic, onion, and bell peppers and sauté for 5 to 10 minutes, until the vegetables are soft. Add the crushed tomato, ketchup, *vino seco*, clam juice, bay leaf, salt, pepper, paprika, and oregano, and bring to a boil. Cover the pot, reduce the heat to low, and simmer for 30 to 40 minutes. Taste the sauce and adjust the seasonings, if necessary.

Raise the heat and bring the sauce to a boil again. Add the shrimp and cook, stirring frequently, for 5 to 10 minutes, until they turn pink. Watch them carefully—it is important not to overcook the shrimp, as this really toughens them. Remove the pot from the heat and let the shrimp sit for a few minutes in the sauce to allow the flavors to penetrate them fully. Remove and discard the bay leaf. Garnish with baby peas and parsley.

Lobster Creole ◆ Langosta Enchilada

This dish is prepared in exactly the same manner as Camarones Enchilados. The only difference is that 6 or 7 medium fresh lobster tails are substituted for the shrimp. To prepare them, cut the tails (shell on) in half. Add the lobsters to the sauce (with the shell still attached) when the recipe directs you to add the shrimp, and simmer for 15 to 20 minutes, until the meat is completely opaque. Like shrimp, lobster becomes tough and rubbery when it is overcooked, so watch it carefully!

Seafood Zarzuela ◆ Zarzuela de Mariscos

A *zarzuela* is a Spanish opera—a fitting name for this delectable dish, since it is truly a symphony of flavors.

Serves 6 to 8

¼ cup olive oil

½ cup chopped onion

¼ cup chopped green bell pepper

¼ cup chopped red bell pepper

1 teaspoon salt

freshly ground black pepper

4 cloves minced garlic

½ pound fresh squid, cleaned and cut into ¼-inch pieces

¼ cup crushed tomatoes

½ teaspoon sweet paprika

½ cup *vino seco* (dry white cooking wine)

2½ cups low-sodium seafood stock

½ cup clam juice

½ pound medium shrimp, peeled and deveined

½ pound fresh mahimahi or other firm white fish, sliced into ½-inch strips

2 medium or 3 small lobster tails

1 dozen clams, scrubbed

1 dozen mussels, scrubbed and debearded

¼ cup finely chopped fresh parsley leaves

1 tablespoon baby peas

◆ In a large Dutch oven, over medium heat, add the oil. When the oil is hot, add the onions and bell peppers. Season with salt and pepper. Add garlic. Cook until translucent—4 to 6 minutes.

Season the squid with salt and pepper. Add to the onion mixture and sauté for 1 minute. Stir in the crushed tomato and paprika and cook for 3 minutes. Add the wine. Add the seafood stock and clam juice and bring to a boil. Reduce the heat to a simmer and cook for 20 minutes. Season the shrimp, fish, and lobster with salt and pepper and add to the pot. Add the clams along with the mussels to the pot, cover, and cook for about 6 to 8 minutes. Garnish with parsley and peas and serve with crusty bread.

Camarón que se duerme, se lo lleva la corriente.

The shrimp that falls asleep is carried away by the current.*

* You snooze you lose.

Paella Versailles

Paella is perhaps the single most popular dish and the traditional main dish in Spain. No wonder many Cuban restaurants serve it. Spain's influence on Cuban cuisine is well established, and our version of paella is a perfect example.

Serves 6 to 8

3 tablespoons extra virgin olive oil
¼ cup yellow onion, finely chopped
¼ cup green bell pepper, finely chopped
4 cloves garlic, finely minced
8 ounces boneless skinless chicken breasts cut into 1- to 1½-inch cubes
½ pound peeled and deveined shrimp
½ pound fresh squid, cleaned and cut into ¼-inch pieces
1 pound fresh clams, scrubbed
1 pound fresh mussels, scrubbed and debearded
8 ounces fresh mahimahi or other firm white fish
¼ cup *vino seco* (dry white cooking wine)
½ cup crushed tomatoes
½ teaspoon ground cumin
1 teaspoon sweet paprika
½ teaspoon crushed red pepper flakes
6 ounces low-sodium chicken stock
3 ounces clam juice
3 cups cooked Yellow Rice (see recipe, page 143)
¼ cup pimientos, coarsely diced
¼ cup baby peas
¼ cup parsley, finely chopped
salt and pepper to taste

◈ In a large paella pan or large skillet over medium-high heat, add olive oil and cook the onion, bell pepper, and garlic for about 4 to 5 minutes. Add the chicken and cook until lightly browned, about 2 minutes.

Add the shrimp, squid, clams, mussels, and fish, and continue to cook for about 2 minutes more.

Add the wine and cook until the alcohol evaporates, about a minute or 2. Add the crushed tomato, cumin, paprika, red pepper flakes, stock and clam juice and continue cooking seafood for 3 minutes. Add rice, pimientos, and peas and continue cooking for about 2 minutes. Garnish with finely chopped parsley.

Eso no pasaba en Cuba.

That didn't happen in Cuba.

Fried Whole Snapper ◇ Pargo Frito

Making whole fried snapper is always a treat. At the restaurant our patrons love it. They linger around the table for a long time ensuring that not a single morsel goes to waste. Remember always to start with the freshest fish you can find—one that smells like the ocean and has clear eyes. It should not smell overwhelmingly fishy.

Serves 4

1 teaspoon garlic powder

1 teaspoon onion powder

½ teaspoon cumin

½ teaspoon black pepper

1 teaspoon salt or more if needed

3 to 4 cups canola oil

4 whole red snappers, scaled, gutted, and cleaned, head left intact

1 cup all-purpose flour

1 cup Mojo Criollo (see recipe, page 21)

◈ Combine the garlic powder, onion powder, cumin, pepper, and salt in a small bowl. Heat the oil—making sure there is enough for the fish to be completely submerged—in a deep fryer or large, deep frying pan over medium-high heat. Season the fish generously with the spice mixture and then dredge well in the flour, making sure it is lightly coated on all sides. Fry each fish separately, turning once after 4 to 5 minutes. The fish will be ready in 8 to 10 minutes. Transfer the fish to a paper towel–lined plate and continue with the remaining fish. Place the fried fish on a serving platter and top with *mojo*.

Lo que se da, no se quita. What you give you don't take back.

Seafood Gratin ◆ Gratinado de Mariscos

Any dish with the word *gratin* in its name is bound to be delicious. Versailles' Seafood Gratin is especially delicious and very popular among our patrons.

Serves 8 to 10

¼ cup olive oil

¾ cup butter, divided

4 cloves garlic, minced

1 cup all-purpose flour, divided

4 cups water

1 teaspoon salt

1 pound shrimp, peeled and deveined

½ pound small scallops

½ pound fresh codfish or other white fish

¾ cup milk

½ cup chicken broth

¼ cup *vino seco* (dry white cooking wine)

1½ cups shredded parmesan cheese, divided

pinch nutmeg

½ teaspoon salt or more to taste

½ teaspoon ground white pepper

◆ In a large skillet, heat the olive oil and ¼ cup of the butter over medium heat. Add the garlic and cook for 2 to 3 minutes. Add half a cup of the flour and continue cooking over medium heat, stirring frequently for 8 to 10 minutes. Remove from heat and set aside.

Fill a large pot ⅔ of the way with water and a teaspoon of salt and bring to a boil. Add the shrimp, scallops and fish, and simmer for 3 to 4 minutes. Drain and reserve ½ cup of the cooking liquid.

In a heavy saucepan, melt ½ cup butter over low heat. Stir in remaining ½ cup flour. Cook while stirring continuously for 2 to 3 minutes.

Combine the milk, chicken broth, wine, and reserved cooking liquid in a large saucepan and bring to a simmer. Whisk the milk mixture into the flour mixture little by little until completely incorporated. Raise temperature to medium and continue stirring with a whisk until the mixture is thickened. Add 1 cup of the parmesan cheese, nutmeg, and salt and pepper to taste. Add the seafood and stir until just combined. Butter a gratin or casserole dish and pour in the seafood mixture. Top with remaining parmesan cheese. Bake in a 350°F oven for 25 to 30 minutes or until the crust has achieved a golden brown color. Serve immediately.

Cod in Spicy Tomato Sauce ◈ Bacalao a la Vizcaína

This recipe is particularly popular during Lent and utilizes salt cod as its main ingredient. It is savory and quite delicious. Get started on this recipe at least a day in advance, because you'll have to soak your salt cod for at least twelve hours before cooking it.

Serves 6

1½ pounds salt cod

½ cup olive oil

5 garlic cloves, minced

2 large onions, chopped

1 medium green bell pepper, chopped

1 medium red bell pepper, chopped

3 cups crushed tomatoes

½ cup *vino seco* (dry white cooking wine)

2 bay leaves

2 tablespoons sweet paprika

1 teaspoon bijol (yellow coloring)

1 teaspoon salt

½ teaspoon white pepper

4 medium to large red potatoes, cut into 2-inch cubes

3 to 4 hard-boiled eggs, sliced, for garnish

½ cup pimientos, for garnish

½ cup peas, for garnish

1 tablespoon Tabasco® sauce (optional)

◈ Place the cod in a large bowl and add cool water to cover. Let the cod soak at room temperature for 10 to 12 hours, changing the water every 1 to 2 hours.

Drain the cod and put it in a large pot. Fill the pot three-quarters full with water and bring to a boil. Boil uncovered for 5 to 10 minutes, then reduce the heat to low, cover the pot, and cook for 10 minutes. Reserve 2 cups of the cod cooking water, then drain the cod, discarding the remaining water. Set the cod aside to cool completely.

Heat ¼ cup of the olive oil in a large frying pan over medium-high heat. Cut the cod into large (2- to 3-inch) chunks; remove any bones. Carefully place the fish in the hot oil and fry it for 2 to 3 minutes per side, until it turns a light golden color. Transfer the fish to a paper towel–lined plate and set aside.

In the same pot used to boil the cod, heat the remaining ¼ cup of the olive oil over medium heat. Add the garlic, onions, and bell peppers and sauté for 10 to 12 minutes, until the vegetables soften and the onion and garlic attain a light golden hue. Add the crushed tomato, *vino seco*, bay leaves, paprika, bijol, salt, and pepper. Raise the heat to high and bring the mixture to a boil, stirring frequently. Let the mixture boil for 3 to 5 minutes, reduce the heat to low, add the potatoes and the reserved cooking liquid, and cover. Cook for 25 to 30 minutes, until the potatoes are fork-tender. Add the cod and stir, incorporating it completely into the sauce.

To serve, spoon the fish stew onto a plate and garnish with hard-boiled eggs, pimientos, peas, and Tabasco® sauce.

SALUD,

Health,

PORQUE

because beauty

BELLEZA

abounds.

SOBRA.

CHICKEN DISHES

The wonderful thing about chicken is that it is truly a blank canvas for all the great flavors that the Cuban *sazón* (seasoning) can impart. Fricasé de Pollo is a classic, as is Arroz con Pollo—but something as simple as Pollo Asado, roast chicken, is escalated to super-yum status by marinating the chicken in *mojo* first. It's hard to mess up a Cuban dish when it's marinated in *mojo*. If you're watching your weight, as many of Versailles' health-conscious patrons are, nothing beats the Pechuga de Pollo a la Plancha, grilled chicken breast. Almost every dish is made better with the addition of garlic or a good *sofrito*. This chapter boasts simple recipes with accessible ingredients, and the flavors will please the whole family.

Fried Chicken Chicharones ◆ Chicharones de Pollo

Forget those frozen chicken fingers; the Versailles *chicharones* are something to write home about. They are golden brown, crispy, and bursting with so much flavor that they won't require any dipping sauce at all. Feel free to use boneless chicken breast to make them more kid friendly. (*Chicharones* are technically pork rinds; this chicken dish is similar to homemade pork rinds in texture and crispiness.)

Serves 4 to 6

2 pounds bone-in, skin-on, chicken
   breast or thighs, cut into 2-inch pieces
¾ cup Mojo Criollo (see recipe, page 21)
½ teaspoon salt (or more, to taste)
½ teaspoon black pepper
1 cup flour
1½ teaspoon salt (for flour mixture)
vegetable oil (for frying)

◆ Place chicken in a glass bowl or large resealable bag and pour *mojo* evenly over the chicken breasts. Allow to marinate, refrigerated, at least 4 hours or overnight. Remove the chicken from the *mojo*, pat dry, and season the chicken with salt and black pepper. Roll the chicken pieces in the flour and salt and place in the refrigerator for at least 1 hour.

In a large heavy skillet, heat the oil to medium heat. Add the chicken pieces and cook, turning once, for approximately 2 to 3 minutes per side, making sure not to crowd the pan. The color should be very light. Drain on paper towels. This can be done as much as 4 hours in advance. When ready to serve, heat the oil again but this time to medium-high heat. Fry the chicken pieces again for a minute or two per side until a deeper golden color is attained. Remove and drain on paper towels. Serve immediately.

Tip: It is not necessary to fry twice, but doing so does give the chicken extra crunch. If frying once, heat oil to medium and fry for 3 minutes per side. Raise temperature to medium-high and cook an additional 2 minutes, turning once after 1 minute.

From the U.K. Straight to a Piece of Heaven

Whenever my husband and I arrive in Miami from England, the first thing we do is head to Versailles with my abuelitos, sometimes the rest of my familia too! My husband always has chicharones de pollo and I have arroz con pollo imperial. Then it's outside to la ventana for a cafecito, where my granddad has a cigar with my husband. It's like a little piece of heaven and it helps me to connect with the stories about Cuba that my granddad tells me.
—Arlene Francis

Grilled Chicken Breast ◈ Pechuga de Pollo a la Plancha

Our figure-conscious patrons order this with a side salad and feel quite virtuous.

Serves 4

2 to 3 tablespoons olive oil
4 boneless, skinless chicken breasts,
  pounded to ¼-inch thickness
1 teaspoon salt

1 teaspoon white pepper
1 teaspoon garlic powder
1 teaspoon onion powder
1 medium onion, thinly sliced (optional)
lime wedges

◈ Heat the olive oil in a large frying pan over medium-high heat. Season chicken breasts liberally with salt, pepper, garlic powder, and onion powder. Add the chicken to the hot oil and sear it for 4 to 5 minutes on each side, until golden brown. Transfer the chicken to a serving dish and cover it with foil to keep it warm.

In the same pan, add the onion and sauté for 3 minutes over medium-high heat, stirring frequently to prevent the onion from burning. Place onions with lime wedges over the chicken breasts and serve immediately.

Chicken Breast Fillets with Garlic ◈ Filetillos de Pollo al Ajillo

This is a delicious and versatile dish, incorporating that Cuban flavor while still being quite simple—a great option for families with small children.

Serves 4

¼ cup olive oil
1 lemon, juiced
4 cloves garlic, crushed and divided
1 teaspoon salt
freshly ground white pepper
4 chicken breast fillets
2 tablespoons butter
all-purpose flour for dredging
¼ cup *vino seco* (dry white cooking wine)
¼ cup low-sodium chicken stock

◈ In a small bowl, whisk together olive oil, lemon juice, 2 cloves of garlic, salt, and pepper. Place chicken in a large bowl, and pour marinade over it. Cover and refrigerate for at least 4 hours.

In a large pan heat butter over medium heat and sauté remaining garlic for 2 to 3 minutes, making certain not to burn it. Drain and pat dry the chicken breasts. *Do not discard marinade.* Dredge chicken in flour and cook breast pieces 4 to 5 minutes per side, depending on thickness, and set aside. Add reserved marinade, wine, and stock to the pan and bring to a boil. Reduce heat and continue cooking for 7 to 8 minutes until thickened and reduced by half. Add chicken back into the pan to heat through and serve with sauce spooned over.

Estás comiendo de lo que pica el pollo.

You are eating what the birds eat.*

*You're wasting your time on foolish things.

Chicken with Yellow Rice ◆ Arroz con Pollo

After black beans, this is perhaps the most requested dish at any Cuban restaurant. It is a great one-dish meal that the whole family will enjoy.

Serves 6 to 8

¼ cup olive oil

1 whole chicken, cut into 8 pieces, or 4 or 5 large, bone-in skinless chicken breasts

3 garlic cloves, minced

1 large onion, chopped

1 medium green bell pepper, chopped

1 (8-ounce) can crushed tomatoes

1 tablespoon bijol

1 bay leaf

1 teaspoon cumin

1 teaspoon dried oregano

1 cup *vino seco* (dry white cooking wine), or 1 (12-ounce) can beer

1 cup Valencia or other short-grain rice

1 cup converted rice

4 cups low-sodium chicken stock

½ teaspoon white pepper

salt to taste

1 (8.5-ounce) can peas (do not drain)

1 small can pimientos

◆ Preheat the oven to 325°F.

Heat the olive oil in a large Dutch oven or ovenproof pot over medium to medium-high heat. Season the chicken generously with salt and pepper, then add it to the pot in batches and sear it, skin side down, for 3 to 5 minutes, until lightly browned. Do not remove too quickly, as it will stick. Be careful not to crowd the pan. (Putting too many pieces of chicken in the pot at once will cause the heat to dissipate, and you'll end up with steamed chicken.) Transfer the chicken to a plate and set aside.

Add the garlic, onion, and bell pepper to the same pot and sauté for about 10 minutes, until soft. Add the tomato and let it simmer for 5 minutes. Add the bijol seasoning, bay leaf, cumin, oregano, and *vino seco*, and cook for 5 more minutes. Add the rice and stir until it is fully incorporated into the tomato mixture. Add 3 cups of stock and the liquid from the canned peas, and stir. Add the chicken and top with as much of the remaining stock as your pot will allow while leaving about 3 inches of space at the top of the pot. Bring to a boil, cover, and reduce the heat to low. Cook for 10 to 15 minutes.

Transfer the entire pot, lid and all, to the oven. (If your pot has a plastic knob, wrap it in foil to protect it from the oven's heat.) Bake for at least 40 minutes, until the rice is uniformly cooked. The liquid need not be fully absorbed for the rice to be ready. You can cook this for longer, depending on how soupy (or *a la chorrera*) you like it. Remember that the liquid continues to evaporate with the residual heat, even out of the oven, so take it out when it is a little soupier than you want it to be. Remove and discard the bay leaf. Adjust seasoning to taste. Decorate the top of the rice with the peas and pimientos.

Chicken Breast Milanese ◈ Pollo a la Milanesa

What could be better than a crispy fried tender boneless breast of chicken topped with marinara sauce and cheese and broiled to perfection? Your whole family will love this chicken. It also makes a great sandwich between two pieces of toasted Cuban bread.

Serves 4

1 tablespoon garlic powder

1 tablespoon onion powder

1 teaspoon salt

½ teaspoon white pepper

4 boneless and skinless chicken breasts, pounded to ¼-inch thickness

¼ cup olive oil

¼ cup all-purpose flour

¾ cup finely ground cracker meal

salt and pepper

4 eggs, beaten

¾ cup prepared (store-bought) marinara sauce

8 ounces shredded mozzarella cheese

2 ounces grated parmesan cheese

◈ Combine the garlic powder, onion powder, salt, and white pepper. Season the chicken breasts generously with this mixture and set aside for at least 1 hour to allow the seasoning to take hold.

Heat the olive oil in a large frying pan over medium-high heat. Combine the flour with the cracker meal in a shallow plate and set aside.

Season the chicken liberally with salt and pepper, then dip it in egg, and then in the flour mixture. Dip the chicken a second time in the egg, then the flour mixture. Shake off any excess and gently lay the chicken in the hot oil. Fry for 4 to 5 minutes on each side, until golden brown. Transfer the chicken to a paper towel–lined platter.

On a cookie sheet or shallow roasting pan, place the chicken breasts in a single layer. Add 2 tablespoons of marinara sauce to each, followed by 2 ounces of the shredded mozzarella cheese and ½ ounce of the parmesan cheese. Place in the oven under the broiler on high for 2–3 minutes or until bubbling and golden brown.

El haragán trabaja doble.

The lazy person works twice as hard.

Chicken and Rice Casserole ◆ Arroz Imperial

If you've never had Arroz Imperial, you're in for a real treat. It's Arroz con Pollo (Chicken with Yellow Rice) with a twist. Arroz Imperial is basically Arroz con Pollo in casserole form. It's like a lasagna—layers of rice and chicken are finished off with a thin coat of mayonnaise. Tangy and delicious!

Serves 6 to 8

¼ cup olive oil

1 large onion, diced

1 medium green bell pepper, diced

3 garlic cloves, minced

1½ cups crushed tomatoes

¼ cup *vino seco* (dry white cooking wine)

1 bay leaf

1 whole chicken, roasted, bones and skin removed, and hand-shredded

3½ cups low-sodium chicken stock

1½ teaspoon bijol

2 cups long grain white rice

salt and pepper

1 cup mayonnaise

4 to 6 hard-boiled eggs sliced in half, for garnish

pimientos and peas, for garnish

◆ Preheat the oven to 375°F.

Heat the olive oil in a large saucepan over medium heat. Add the onion, bell pepper, and garlic, and sauté for 5 to 7 minutes, until the onions are translucent. Be careful not to brown the vegetables. Add the tomato, *vino seco*, and bay leaf, and cook for another 5 minutes. Add the chicken, stir well, and cook for 3 minutes. Remove from the heat and set aside. Remove and discard the bay leaf.

Bring the stock to a boil over high heat in a large saucepan. Add the bijol and rice, and bring the mixture to a boil again. Cook, uncovered, for 5 minutes. Reduce the heat to low, fluff the rice with a fork, cover the pan, and cook for 17 to 20 minutes, until the rice is tender and fluffy. Taste the rice and season with salt and pepper to taste.

Grease the bottom and sides of a 3-quart rectangular casserole dish. Spread a thin layer of rice in the dish, about ¼-inch thick, then add a layer of the chicken mixture. Spread half the remaining rice on top of the chicken, then spread the remaining chicken mixture on top of that. Top the layers with the remaining rice.

Spread the mayonnaise evenly across the top of the casserole. Garnish with eggs, pimientos, and peas.

Tip: You may also boil a whole chicken and shred it to add to the *sofrito*. Save the liquid in which it was boiled and use it in place of the boxed stock. You will have to adjust salt in this dish if you use this method. Some of our patrons request melted mozzarella cheese on top, which is a delicious variation.

Shredded Chicken with Onions ◈ Vaca Frita de Pollo

Vaca Frita de Pollo is a new and super-popular dish at our restaurant, and really delicious. The delicate flavor of chicken is the perfect foil for the flavors of citrus and onion. It is favored by our patrons who are limiting their red meat intake.

Serves 6

2 pounds chicken breasts bone-in, or whole chicken
3 teaspoons salt
1 bay leaf
1 tablespoon garlic powder
1 tablespoon onion powder
1 teaspoon salt
½ teaspoon white pepper
4 tablespoons light olive oil
2 medium yellow onions, preferably sweet Vidalia, sliced thinly
white vinegar

Te ahogas en un vaso de agua.

You drown in a glass of water.

◈ Using a stockpot, add chicken and cold water to cover, reaching about 2 inches above the chicken. Add 3 teaspoons of salt and bay leaf, and bring to a boil on medium-high heat. Reduce heat to medium-low, cover, and let it simmer for about 50 minutes to an hour, or until meat is tender and falls off the bones.

Carefully remove chicken from stockpot. After chicken has cooled, debone and shred by hand. The finer the shred, the crispier the finished product. Season the chicken with the garlic powder, onion powder, 1 teaspoon salt, and white pepper.

Heat a large skillet to medium-high and add the oil; once oil is hot, add the shredded chicken and sauté for about 3 minutes. Add the thinly sliced onion and cook on medium-high, stirring constantly, until chicken turns golden brown and onions are translucent and soft. Drizzle a touch of white vinegar to finish dish and serve immediately.

Tip: To make this dish you may also use rotisserie chicken with excellent results.

Roast Chicken ◆ Pollo Asado

This simple dish is a joy to make because it is effortless and fills your home with a delicious aroma. The leftovers are perfect for our delectable Ensalada de Pollo (see recipe, page 61).

Serves 6

3 tablespoons white vinegar
8 garlic cloves, minced
¼ cup olive oil
1 tablespoon sweet paprika
1 teaspoon cumin
1 teaspoon dried oregano
2 medium onions, thinly sliced
1 bay leaf
Salt and white pepper
1 (5- to 7-pound) whole roaster chicken
4 tablespoons salted butter
½ cup *vino seco* (dry white cooking wine)
½ cup low-sodium chicken stock
1 tablespoon Kitchen Bouquet®

◆ Combine the vinegar, garlic, oil, dry spices, onion, bay leaf, and salt and pepper to taste in a bowl.

Pour the vinegar-based marinade over the chicken, cover it tightly with plastic wrap, and refrigerate for at least 8 hours or overnight.

Preheat the oven to 375°F. Lightly coat a large roasting pan with olive oil. Remove the chicken from the marinade, reserving the marinade, and place the chicken breast side up in the roasting pan. Rub the top and sides of the chicken with 2 tablespoons of the butter.

Roast the chicken for 1½ to 2 hours, depending on the size of the chicken (allow 20 minutes per pound). You may cover the pan very loosely with foil for the first hour of roasting to prevent the breast from drying out, but be sure to remove the foil during the last hour so that the skin browns evenly. Allow the chicken to stand for at least 15 minutes before carving.

Pour the marinade into a large saucepan and bring it to a boil. Add pan drippings, wine, stock, and Kitchen Bouquet® and bring to a boil. Continue boiling for 10 to 15 minutes or until marinade is reduced by half and is slightly thickened. Add the 2 additional tablespoons of butter at the very end of the cooking process, as this will act as a thickening agent. Pour over the chicken and serve.

Chicken Fricassee ◈ Fricasé de Pollo

This dish is another of the many tomato-based wonders that Cubans enjoy. This is also great the day after it is cooked, making for fantastic leftovers. While the traditional recipe calls for a whole chicken cut up, feel free to use only white or dark meat if that is your preference.

Serves 6

½ cup olive oil

1 tablespoon salt

1 teaspoon pepper

6 large chicken breasts, bone-in and skin on, or 1 (5- to 7-pound) whole fryer chicken, cut into 8 pieces

4 garlic cloves, minced

1 large onion, chopped

1 medium green bell pepper, chopped

2 cups crushed tomatoes

1 cup low-sodium chicken stock

1 teaspoon bijol (yellow coloring)

½ cup *vino seco* (dry white cooking wine)

1 bay leaf

1 teaspoon ground cumin

1 teaspoon dried oregano

6 small red potatoes, peeled and cut in half

½ cup pimiento-stuffed olives

◈ Heat half of the olive oil in a large heavy pot over medium-high heat. Season the chicken with the salt and pepper, then add it to the pot and sear it for 4 to 5 minutes, until the outside of the chicken pieces turns light golden brown. Transfer the chicken to a plate and set aside.

Heat the remaining olive oil in the pot. Add the garlic, onion, and bell pepper, and sauté for 10 to 12 minutes, until the onion slightly caramelizes. Add the crushed tomatoes, stock, bijol, *vino seco*, bay leaf, cumin, and oregano, and bring to a boil. Add the chicken, cover the pot, and reduce the heat to low and cook for 30 minutes. Add the potatoes and cook an additional 30 minutes.

Add the olives and stir well. Taste and adjust the seasonings, if necessary. Remove and discard the bay leaf.

Every pig
A CADA CERDO
eventually
LE LLEGA SU
meets his
NOCHEBUENA.
Christmas Eve.

PORK DISHES

When you think about Cuban food, what comes to mind first? Okay, after black beans. Pork, naturally! Yup, we love our pork, and if you are looking for a little or a lot of pork, then follow us to Versailles. Cubans seem to add pork to everything! Our Cuban sandwich has pork of course, but so do our omelets—in the form of chorizo—and even our steak sandwiches can be ordered with ham. So if you love your pork, you have come to the right place. Let's embark on this culinary journey together. Your senses will not be disappointed.

Pork is the focal point of Cuban cuisine. Whole roasted pigs are the centerpiece of many celebrations, and all Cuban men are experts in swine and the many methods for cooking it. Fortunately, you will not need any special equipment to indulge in the delicious recipes in this chapter—no *caja china* (roasting box) or pit in the ground required. This chapter is full of easy and delicious recipes that our customers order again and again. Most of the recipes involve our beloved *mojo*, which makes pork in particular sing when combined with traditional Cuban spices like garlic, cumin, and oregano. These recipes truly celebrate our love of pork.

Four Decades of Tradition for This Cubanita!

As a child, I visited Versailles when we vacationed in Miami. It was almost a tradition—something that was a must! I don't know why, but I was always astonished by all the conversations taking place simultaneously outside. I was just a kid, and I guess I had never seen so much activity by a little window. What was so magical about this place? People drank coffee in tiny paper cups. El cafecito took almost as long as the whole meal—it was just weird to understand!

As I grew older, Miami became a place to go to concerts and Coconut Grove in addition to visiting family. The trips to Versailles continued, except now they were much later in the evening. By then both Versailles and I had grown! I always felt such a strong connection to this place even though I was not a local.

I visited during its fortieth anniversary and I was having so much fun singing along at my table that I was asked to get up and join in! This was, by far, the most fun I've ever had at my favorite place in Miami! Versailles and I are both in our forties and going strong!
—Marissa Cuervo-Cipriano

Roast Pork ◈ Lechón Asado

We love this recipe because it is so low maintenance. You virtually ignore it once you get it in the oven. This pork cooks slowly in your oven for up to seven hours, after marinating for the preceding twenty-four hours. So be forewarned.

Serves 10 to 12

½ cup grapefruit juice
½ cup lime juice
¼ cup white vinegar
15 garlic cloves, minced
2 medium onions, thinly sliced
1 tablespoon dried oregano
1 tablespoon ground cumin
2 teaspoons white pepper
4 tablespoons coarse salt
1 (8- to 10-pound) pork shoulder
3 tablespoons olive oil

◈ Combine the grapefruit juice, lime juice, vinegar, garlic, onions, oregano, cumin, pepper, and 1 tablespoon of the salt in a large bowl.

Rinse and dry the pork, then rub it all over with the remaining 2 tablespoons of salt. Place the pork skin side up in a high-sided roasting pan that will fit in your refrigerator. Pour half the juice mixture around the pork, being careful not to wet the skin; cover it with foil, and refrigerate for 8 hours or overnight. Do not turn, as skin must be dry. Keep remaining marinade refrigerated in an airtight container.

Preheat the oven to 400°F.

Rub olive oil on pork skin. Bake skin side up, for 30 minutes. Then reduce the heat to 275°F and cover with foil and let the pork roast for at least 5 hours, or up to 7 hours. It must register 170° when a meat thermometer is inserted in the thickest part of the pork.

Two hours before serving, remove the foil and increase the oven temperature to 375°F. Continue roasting the pork for 1 more hour.

Remove the pork from the oven and let it stand in the pan for 30 minutes. While the pork rests, bring the reserved marinade to a boil in a small saucepan. Boil for 3 to 5 minutes, until the garlic softens.

To serve, carve the roast—although most of the time, carving won't be necessary, as the meat will just fall off the bone—and pour the warmed marinade over the pork.

Fried Pork Chunks ◇ Masas de Puerco Frita

Is there anything better or more representative of Cuban cuisine than fried pork? Probably not. After all, it is the marriage of two of our favorite things: pork and frying.

Serves 6–8

2½ pounds pork shoulder
1 teaspoon dried oregano
1 teaspoon cumin
½ teaspoon black pepper
1 teaspoon sweet paprika
4 cloves garlic, minced
1 bay leaf
1 cup lime juice
2 cups lightly salted water
¼ cup lard or vegetable oil
½ teaspoon salt
½ onion, sliced into rings
1 lime, cut in wedges

◇ Cut pork into 2-inch chunks and set aside. Combine all ingredients except lime wedges and onions to create a marinade. Cover the pork chunks with marinade. Marinate for at least 4 hours or overnight in the refrigerator.

Remove meat from marinade and pat dry with a paper towel. Place the meat in a pot with 2 cups of lightly salted water and lard or vegetable oil. Bring to a boil, reduce heat to low, and simmer, uncovered, until all water boils away—about 30 to 45 minutes.

Lightly brown the cooked pork in the melted fat until crispy on the outside. Toss in the onion slices and sauté briefly. Garnish with lime wedges.

Grilled Pork Chops ◆ Chuletas de Puerco

If you don't want to indulge in fried pork or take the time to make a whole leg, this is a great option. It is quick and easy and the perfect main dish to serve alongside black beans and rice.

Serves 4

4 boneless pork loin or rib chops, about 1 inch thick (about 2 pounds)
3 tablespoons olive oil
¼ cup lime juice
¼ cup grapefruit juice
3 tablespoons white vinegar
½ teaspoon black pepper
1 teaspoon salt
1 clove garlic, finely chopped
2 tablespoons olive or vegetable oil
1 large onion, thinly sliced

◆ Combine all ingredients except oil, rub all sides of the chops with this mixture, and allow to marinate for at least 45 minutes and up to 4 hours in the refrigerator.

Heat the olive oil over medium-high heat in a large skillet. Sear each side of the pork chops for about 4 minutes or until golden brown. Remove from heat, add the onions to the skillet, and sauté quickly about 2–3 minutes, adding another teaspoon of oil, if necessary. Place onions over the pork chops and serve immediately.

Breaded Pork Medallions ◆ Medallones de Puerco Empanizado

Serves 4 to 6

2 large eggs
1 cup vegetable oil
1 pound pork tenderloin in 1½ inch slices
salt and black pepper to taste
2 cups seasoned breadcrumbs
¼ cup prepared Mojo Criollo (see recipe, page 21)

◆ Beat eggs in large bowl.

Heat oil in medium frying pan on medium heat. Season pork slices with salt and pepper. Place seasoned breadcrumbs on a large plate. Dip pork steaks in the beaten egg to coat well,

then dredge them in the breadcrumbs, making certain to coat well on all sides.

Fry steaks in oil 4–5 minutes per side, or until golden brown. Drain on paper towel–lined plate and then place in a shallow baking dish.

Place in 350°F oven for 15 to 20 minutes. Meanwhile, in a small skillet reduce the *mojo* by half over medium heat. Pour over pork steaks and serve immediately.

Tip: We like to allow the steaks to sit, uncovered, in the refrigerator for at least 20 minutes before frying, so that the coating adheres well.

Pasta with Ham and Spanish Sausage ◈ Macarrones con Jamón y Chorizo

You won't find too many pasta recipes in a Cuban restaurant, but this is the exception. This pasta includes every Cuban's favorite, pork! A real comfort dish.

Serves 4 to 6

¼ cup olive oil

1 medium onion, chopped

1 garlic clove, minced

1 small red bell pepper, chopped

1 small green bell pepper, chopped

2 cups crushed tomatoes

3 tablespoons *vino seco* (dry white cooking wine)

1 teaspoon dried oregano

1 bay leaf

1 teaspoon salt

½ teaspoon white pepper

½ cup grated parmesan cheese

¾ pound Spanish chorizo sausage, chopped

½ pound ham steak, chopped

1 pound ziti (short tubular pasta)

◈ Heat the olive oil in a large frying pan over medium-high heat. Add the onion, garlic, and the red and green bell peppers, and reduce the heat to medium. Sauté for 5 to 7 minutes, until the onion is translucent. Add the tomato, *vino seco*, oregano, bay leaf, salt and pepper, and cook for 5 minutes. Reduce the heat to low and add the parmesan cheese, chorizo, and ham. Simmer for 5 to 7 minutes, until the sauce has thickened slightly and all the flavors have had an opportunity to meld. Set aside.

Cook the pasta according to the package directions for al dente pasta (do not add oil to the water, but do add salt); drain the pasta. Return the pasta to the pot in which it was cooked and pour the sauce over it. Stir in additional parmesan cheese if desired and taste the pasta; adjust the seasonings if necessary.

Lo que está pa ti nadie te lo quita.

What is destined for you no one can take away.

Tip: This recipe can also be made with prepared (store-bought) marinara sauce with excellent results. Just substitute 2½ cups of your favorite good quality marinara for the crushed tomatoes, onion, garlic, and peppers in this recipe.

a great many ailments can be cured with

UN BISTECSITO

Beef Dishes

Beef is an important part of the Cuban diet. Beef solves a lot of problems. If you are sick, eat beef. If you feel weak, eat a steak. If you need to replenish after the big game, have some Vaca Frita. Anemic? Ropa Vieja is just what the doctor ordered.

Traditionally Cubans believe that without the iron that beef provides, we would all be anemic. Everyone has an uncle, cousin, or distant relative who was or claims to have been a doctor in Cuba. The general consensus is that a great many ailments can be cured with *un bistecsito* (a little steak).

Kidding aside, beef is important to Cubans, and Versailles does beef any way you like it. Our all-time favorite is Ropa Vieja, literally meaning "old clothes"—doesn't sound too appetizing, does it? Yet it's heaven on a plate. Another favorite? Picadillo, which is so versatile. You will see it used several times in this cookbook in things such as Empanadas de Carne. If you love beef, you'll love the recipes in this chapter. If you believe the Cuban lore, you'll feel better and stronger after eating it!

The Stopover

Was flying back from visiting the in-laws in Panama, on our way back to Colorado; had a four-hour layover. What did I want to do? Make a mad dash for Versailles and get some ropa vieja! Heaven!
—*Todd Erlenbusch*

Shredded Fried Beef and Onions, or Fried Cow ◈ Vaca Frita

Technically this dish is exactly what its name says it is—beef that is in fact fried. But as is the case for Ropa Vieja, the translation of this recipe's name does not do the dish justice. This is perfectly seasoned and tender shredded flank steak, fried until slightly crispy, with onions and garlic.

Serves 6 to 8

1 bay leaf
2 pounds flank steak or blade steak
2 teaspoons salt
½ teaspoon white pepper
1 tablespoon garlic powder
1 tablespoon onion powder
¼ cup vegetable oil
2 medium onions, thinly sliced
2 tablespoons white vinegar
cooked white rice
lime wedges, optional

◈ Bring 2 quarts of salted water to a boil in a large stockpot. Add the bay leaf and steak, then reduce the heat, cover the pot, and simmer for 2 hours.

Drain the flank steak and let it cool to room temperature on a plate lined with paper towels. Use your hands to shred the beef into long strips; if you shred it along the grain, it should come apart easily. Season the steak with salt, pepper, garlic powder, and onion powder and place it in a shallow, nonreactive dish and let it marinate for at least 30 minutes.

Preheat a large cast-iron skillet over medium-high heat. Add half the vegetable oil and heat it until it is almost smoking. Add the steak and sauté, stirring frequently, for 7 to 10 minutes. Add the onions and sauté for 5 minutes, until the edges of the beef become crispy. Pour vinegar evenly over beef and cook for another minute. Serve immediately with white rice and lime wedges.

Seasoned Ground Beef Hash ◈ Picadillo

Picadillo is a very traditional Cuban dish that is also extremely versatile. Any leftovers can be used creatively, as in our Empanadas de Carne (turnovers—see recipe, page 33). Many of our patrons order this dish *a caballo* with two fried eggs on top. It's a delicious variation.

Serves 4 to 6

¼ cup olive oil
4 garlic cloves, minced
1 medium onion, chopped
1 small green bell pepper, minced
1 pound ground sirloin or ground round
¼ cup *vino seco* (dry white cooking wine)
½ cup crushed tomatoes
½ cup low-sodium chicken or beef stock
1 teaspoon dried oregano
1 bay leaf
1 teaspoon ground cumin
salt and pepper to taste
¼ cup raisins
¼ cup pimiento-stuffed olives, roughly chopped
cooked white rice

◈ Heat half the olive oil in a medium-sized shallow pot over medium-high heat. Add the garlic, onion, and bell pepper, and sauté for 5 to 7 minutes, until tender. Raise the heat slightly. Add the beef when the pan is hot and sauté, breaking up any large chunks of meat. Sauté for 10 to 15 minutes, until the beef is thoroughly cooked (no longer red). Drain any excess liquid from the pan.

Add the *vino seco*, crushed tomato, chicken stock, the remaining olive oil, oregano, bay leaf, ground cumin, and salt and pepper to taste. Reduce the heat to low, cover the pot, and simmer for about 20 minutes. Add the raisins and olives and serve over white rice.

Shredded Beef in Tomato Sauce ◈ Ropa Vieja

Ropa Vieja is especially popular with the non-Spanish-speaking set, who seem to enjoy the funny name meaning old clothes. Perhaps they order it because curiosity gets the better of them. This dish is made using shredded flank steak that is boiled long enough to make it extremely tender and then sautéed in a savory *sofrito*-infused tomato sauce and garnished with peas and pimientos.

Serves 6 to 8

2 teaspoons salt, plus more as needed

2 pounds flank steak or blade steak

½ cup vegetable oil

4 garlic cloves, minced

½ cup crushed white onion

2 cups crushed tomatoes

1 bay leaf

½ teaspoon white pepper

1 teaspoon ground cumin

1 teaspoon dried oregano

1 teaspoon sweet paprika

1 teaspoon sugar

1 cup *vino seco* (dry white cooking wine)

1 medium onion, julienne sliced

1 medium green bell pepper, julienne sliced

1 medium red bell pepper, julienne sliced

½ cup canned peas, for garnish

¼ cup chopped pimientos, for garnish

◈ Combine 1½ quarts water and 1 teaspoon of the salt in a large pot and bring to a boil over high heat. Add the steak and reduce the heat to low. Cover the pot and cook for about 2 hours, until the meat is nice and tender.

Heat the vegetable oil in a large frying pan over medium heat. Add the garlic and crushed onion and sauté for 4 to 5 minutes. Add the crushed tomato, bay leaf, pepper, cumin, oregano, paprika, sugar, and remaining teaspoon of salt, and bring the mixture to a boil. Add the *vino seco* and continue boiling for 5 minutes. Add the bell peppers and sliced onions, reduce the heat to low and simmer for 20 minutes. Remove the pan from the heat and set aside.

Drain the flank steak and let it cool to room temperature on a plate lined with paper towels. Use your hands to shred the beef into long strips; if you shred it along the grain, it should come apart easily. Season the steak with salt and pepper and add it to the tomato mixture. Stir to coat the meat with the sauce. Cook over medium-low heat for a minimum of 20 to 30 minutes, to allow the flavors to come together. Remove and discard the bay leaf. Garnish with peas and pimientos before serving.

Cuban-Style Pot Roast ◈ Carne Asada

This is the Cuban version of pot roast, and what makes it uniquely Cuban is the flavor that only a good *sofrito* can add. This is made using a tougher cut of meat, which is cooked low and slow until fork-tender.

Serves 6 to 8

4 pounds tip beef or London broil
½ cup vegetable oil
1 large yellow onion, chopped
4 cloves of garlic, minced
1 medium green bell pepper, chopped
1½ cups low-sodium beef stock
1 (8-ounce) can crushed tomatoes
1 teaspoon dried oregano
1 teaspoon ground cumin
1 cup *vino seco* (dry white cooking wine)
salt and pepper to taste

◈ Season beef generously with salt and pepper. Heat the oil in a large dutch oven and brown the roast on all sides.

When the roast is browned, remove from pot and set aside.

Place the onions, garlic, and bell pepper in the same pot and cook them for 5–6 minutes or until translucent.

Place roast back in pot and cover it with beef stock, tomato, remaining spices, and *vino seco*. Cook over low heat, covered, for 1½ to 2 hours.

Remove from heat and adjust seasoning, adding more salt and pepper if necessary.

Slice the beef thinly, across the grain, and pour sauce over it. Serve immediately.

Breaded Fried Steak ◆ Bistec Empanizado

Bistec Empanizado is like chicken-fried steak but better, because it is first marinated with Versailles' famous citrusy Cuban spice. The breaded steaks served at the restaurant are so large that they encompass a whole plate!

Serves 4

¼ cup sour orange juice, or a mixture of equal parts lime juice and grapefruit juice
4 garlic cloves, minced
4 (¼-inch-thick) sirloin steaks (minute steaks)
salt and pepper
vegetable oil, for shallow frying
4 eggs, beaten
¾ cup finely ground cracker meal
¼ cup all-purpose flour
lime wedges, for serving

◆ Combine the sour orange juice and garlic in a small bowl.

Arrange the steaks in a shallow, non-reactive dish and pour the orange juice and garlic over them. Cover the steaks with plastic wrap and marinate them in the refrigerator for 1 hour. Drain the steaks, pat them dry, and season them liberally with salt and pepper.

Heat the vegetable oil in a large frying pan over medium-high heat. Place the eggs in a shallow bowl. Combine the cracker meal and flour in another shallow bowl. Dip the steaks in the egg, then in the flour mixture. Repeat this step, dipping the steaks in the egg and flour mixture a second time. Shake off any excess flour and gently lay the steaks in the hot oil. Fry each steak individually for about 3 minutes each side, until golden brown. Transfer the steaks to a paper towel–lined platter to drain. Serve immediately with wedges of lime.

Milanese-Style Steak ◆ Bistec a la Milanesa

This is a delicious twist on Bistec Empanizado (Breaded Fried Steak) with the addition of tangy marinara sauce and melted cheese. Delicious served with our mashed potatoes!

Serves 4

4 (¼-inch-thick) sirloin steaks (minute steaks
1 teaspoon salt
1 tablespoon garlic powder
1 tablespoon onion powder
½ teaspoon white pepper
vegetable oil, for shallow frying
4 eggs, beaten
¾ cup finely ground cracker meal
¼ cup all-purpose flour
1 cup prepared (store-bought) marinara sauce
1 cup shredded mozzarella cheese
¼ cup grated parmesan cheese

◈ Combine the salt, pepper, garlic powder, and onion powder in a small bowl.

Arrange the steaks in a shallow, non-reactive dish and season generously with the spice mix. Cover the steaks with plastic wrap and place them in the refrigerator for 30 minutes.

Heat the vegetable oil in a large frying pan over medium-high heat. Place the eggs in a shallow bowl. Combine the cracker meal and flour in another shallow bowl. Dip the steaks in the egg, then in the flour mixture. Repeat this step, dipping the steaks in the egg and flour mixture a second time. Shake off any excess flour and gently lay the steaks in the hot oil. Fry each steak individually for about 3 minutes on each side, until golden brown. Transfer the steaks to a paper towel–lined platter to drain.

Preheat the broiler. Place the steaks on a baking sheet. Spread 4 tablespoons of marinara sauce on top of each steak, then sprinkle each with mozzarella cheese and then with parmesan cheese. Broil the steaks for 2 to 3 minutes, until the cheese starts to bubble and turn a light golden color. Serve immediately.

Grilled Steak ◈ Palomilla

We can hardly keep count of how many *palomilla* steaks we serve at the restaurant. Premium steak, simple Cuban seasoning, and the right temperature are the secrets to perfecting this dish.

Serves 4

1 teaspoon salt
½ teaspoon white pepper
1 tablespoon garlic powder
1 tablespoon onion powder
4 (¼-inch-thick) sirloin steaks (minute steaks)
2 tablespoons vegetable oil
1 cup chopped onion
¼ cup chopped parsley
lime wedges (optional)

◈ Combine the salt, pepper, garlic powder, and onion powder in a small bowl.

Arrange the steaks in a shallow, nonreactive dish and season generously with the spice mixture. Set aside the steaks at room temperature for 15 to 30 minutes. Heat 1 tablespoon of the vegetable oil in a cast-iron pan until the oil is almost smoking. Carefully fry the steaks, one at a time, for about 2 minutes on each side. Transfer the cooked steak to a plate and continue with the remaining steaks, letting the pan return to a high temperature after each steak. Add the remaining tablespoon of olive oil to the pan before frying the third and fourth steaks.

Combine the onion and parsley in a small bowl. Garnish each steak with the onion-parsley mixture and lime wedges.

Plantain Pie with Picadillo ◆ Pastel de Plátano

This dish is a uniquely Cuban delight. It is layered and baked like a lasagna, but mashed sweet plantains are the base of this delicious dish. With a layer of melted cheese it is sweet, savory, and meaty all in one bite.

Serves 6 to 8

1 teaspoon sugar

3 very ripe plantains, skin removed, and sliced into 1-inch pieces

½ teaspoon salt

½ teaspoon bijol (yellow coloring)

1 pound prepared *picadillo* (see recipe, page 103)

1½ cups shredded mozzarella cheese

¼ cup grated parmesan cheese

cooked white rice

◆ Preheat oven to 350°F.

Bring a large pot filled two-thirds with water to a boil over medium-high heat. Add the sugar and the sliced plantains. Reduce heat to medium-low. Cover and continue cooking until plantains are soft and tender, about 30 to 45 minutes, depending on the ripeness of the plantain. Remove from heat and drain. Mash the plantains by hand or preferably in a food processor with salt and bijol.

Heat the *picadillo* and then drain it to avoid excessive liquid. In a large shallow nonstick baking pan spread half of the plantain purée evenly. Then spread the *picadillo* evenly on top of it. Top the *picadillo* with remaining layer of plantain purée. Top with mozzarella and parmesan cheese. Bake in oven for 20 to 25 minutes or until cheese is bubbling and golden brown. Allow to stand for approximately 10 minutes before cutting into squares and serving. Serve with white rice and extra *picadillo* on the side.

Catalonian Meatballs ◆ Albondigas

Meatballs have now become widely popular, but these delicious balls of goodness have been on our menu for decades and remain a favorite among our long-term guests as well as the newer fans. This recipe's origin is the Catalonian region of Spain.

Serves 6

2 pounds ground beef

3 cloves garlic, crushed and chopped

1 tablespoon garlic powder

2 large eggs, beaten

¼ cup dry breadcrumbs soaked in
   ¼ cup milk

1 teaspoon salt

½ teaspoon black pepper

1 teaspoon ground cumin

⅓ cup raisins

¼ cup vegetable oil

1 yellow onion, finely chopped

1 medium green bell pepper, finely
   chopped

1 tablespoon tomato paste

1 cup crushed tomatoes

1 cup low-sodium chicken stock

2 tablespoons fresh parsley, chopped

2 pimientos, chopped

◆ Gently mix the ground beef, garlic, garlic powder, eggs, breadcrumb mixture, salt, pepper, cumin, and raisins. Form 1-inch meatballs with the mixture and set them aside.

Heat the vegetable oil in a large Dutch oven. Add the meatballs, in batches, and sauté them until they turn brown. Remove them from the heat and set aside.

Add the chopped onions and bell peppers to the skillet and sauté them for 5 minutes, until they turn soft and light brown. Add tomato paste, cooking for another 3 minutes. Add the crushed tomatoes and cook 5 minutes more. Pour the chicken stock over the onion and tomato mixture and stir until smooth.

Return meatballs to pot. Cover with the lid and cook the mixture over low heat for 30 minutes, until the meatballs are cooked through and the juices run clear. Serve the meatballs and sauce over rice, and sprinkle with parsley and chopped pimientos.

Tira la piedra y esconde la mano.

He throws the stone and hides his hand.

Oxtail Stew ◈ Rabo Encendido

The literal translation of the name of this dish is "tail on fire." Oxtail, when cooked properly, is tender and succulent with a rich red gravy and flavor that keep people ordering it again and again.

Serves 6 to 8

3 pounds oxtails, trimmed of all visible fat and cut into 2-inch pieces
salt and pepper
all-purpose flour, for dredging
3 tablespoons olive oil
4 garlic cloves, minced
2 cups onion, diced
1 cup green bell pepper, diced
2 cups crushed tomatoes
1 cup dry red wine
¼ cup *vino seco* (dry white cooking wine)
1 cup low-sodium beef stock
1 bay leaf
½ teaspoon dried oregano
½ teaspoon ground cumin
1 teaspoon salt
½ teaspoon pepper
1 tablespoon vinegar
½ cup pimiento-stuffed olives
chopped parsley, for garnish

Mejor solo que mal acompañado.

Better alone than in bad company.

◈ Season the oxtails with salt and pepper, dredge them lightly in flour, and set them aside.

Heat the olive oil in a large heavy-bottomed pot over medium-high heat. Add the oxtails in small batches and sear them on all sides. Transfer the seared oxtails to a plate and set them aside.

Reduce the heat to medium and add the garlic, onion, and bell pepper. Sauté for 5 to 7 minutes, until the vegetables are tender. Add the crushed tomatoes and continue cooking for another 5 minutes. Add the red wine, *vino seco*, stock, bay leaf, oregano, cumin, salt, pepper, and vinegar and increase the heat to medium-high. Bring it to a slow boil. Add the oxtails, reduce the heat to low, cover the pot, and let the stew simmer for 2 hours.

Add the olives and continue cooking covered for an additional 45 minutes to 1 hour, until the meat is falling off the bones. Taste the stew and adjust the seasonings, adding more salt and pepper if necessary. Remove and discard the bay leaf. Garnish with chopped parsley.

Meatloaf ◆ Pulpeta

This is no ordinary meatloaf. It is not even close to the gray-hued, crumbly dry brick that may spring to mind. This is meatloaf Cuban style, so it is moist and flavorful. It is slowly simmered in a delicious tangy tomato sauce infused with garlic, bell pepper, and onion.

Serves 6 to 8

1 pound ground sirloin

½ pound ground pork

½ pound ground sweet ham, such as honey- or maple-glazed ham (see note below)

2 teaspoons salt

1 teaspoon pepper

1 teaspoon dried oregano, divided

1 teaspoon sweet paprika, divided

1 egg, beaten

1 cup cracker meal

½ cup olives, sliced

½ cup olive oil

4 garlic cloves, minced

1 medium green bell pepper, diced

1 large yellow onion, diced

1 cup crushed tomatoes

1 bay leaf

¼ cup *vino seco* (dry white cooking wine)

½ teaspoon ground cumin

½ cup canned peas (reserve liquid)

½ cup pimientos

◆ Combine the beef, pork, and ham in a large bowl. Add 1 teaspoon of the salt, ½ teaspoon each of the pepper, oregano, and paprika. Knead the meat lightly by hand until all the ingredients are thoroughly combined. Add the egg and half of the cracker meal, and mix until thoroughly combined.

Transfer the meat mixture to a baking sheet and use your hands to shape it into one or two oblong or rectangular loaves. If this if your first time making this meatloaf, you might try making two loaves instead of one, as it's a little easier. Create wells in the center of the loaf: four wells if making one loaf, or two each if making two loaves. Carefully place the sliced olives in the wells and cover them. Sprinkle the loaf or loaves with the remaining cracker crumbs to create a light coating, then pat the crumbs so that they stick. Cover each loaf with plastic wrap, transfer the baking sheet to the refrigerator, and refrigerate for 1 hour.

Just before you take the meatloaf out of the refrigerator, heat the olive oil in a large pot over medium-high heat. Add the garlic, bell pepper, and onion, and sauté for about 10 minutes, until the vegetables are soft. Add the tomatoes, bay leaf, *vino seco*, the remaining oregano and paprika, cumin, the remaining salt and pepper, and ¼ cup of the reserved pea liquid. Bring to a boil and cook for 5 minutes. Reduce the heat to low, cover the pot, and let the mixture simmer for 30 to 45 minutes.

While that cooks, remove the meatloaf from the refrigerator to let it warm up a bit.

Coat a large, shallow frying pan with nonstick cooking spray or olive or vegetable oil and heat over medium-high heat. Carefully transfer the meatloaf to the pan and sear it on all sides, creating a golden crust. It is not necessary to cook the meat all the way through, just enough for it to firm up and remain stable.

Gently place the browned meatloaf in the pot with the tomato sauce mixture. Cover the pot, set the heat to medium-low, and cook for 45 minutes to 1 hour. Spoon the sauce over the meat occasionally, but do not stir.

Carefully transfer the meat to a large platter and let it rest about 10 minutes before cutting it into slices. To serve, pour tomato mixture over each serving and garnish with peas and pimientos.

Tip: To make ground ham, buy sliced ham from the deli and pulse it in the food processor until it is finely ground.

Pot Roast ◆ Boliche

This delicious roast beef is made extra special with the addition of Spanish chorizo. This is one of those dishes that is even more delicious the next day. Boliche tastes great cold or at room temperature.

Makes 8 or more servings

1 (3-pound) eye of round roast
2 small Spanish-style chorizo sausages
1 teaspoon salt
½ teaspoon white pepper
¼ cup olive oil
1 large onion, chopped
4 garlic cloves, minced
1 green bell pepper, chopped
1 cup *vino seco* (dry white cooking wine)
1 cup crushed tomatoes
¾ cup beef stock
1 teaspoon ground cumin
1 teaspoon dried oregano
1 bay leaf
1 tablespoon Kitchen Bouquet®
2 tablespoons chopped parsley

◆ Using a long sharp knife, create a slit on each end (in the center) of the roast wide enough to accommodate the chorizo. Remove the casings from the chorizo and stuff the chorizo carefully into the slit in the meat. Generously season the meat with salt and pepper. In a large pot or Dutch oven, heat the olive oil over medium-high heat and sear the meat on all sides until lightly brown. Set aside.

Reduce the heat to medium and cook the onions, garlic, and bell peppers for 5 to 7 minutes, or until translucent. Place the beef back in the pot, add the wine, tomatoes, stock, cumin, oregano, bay leaf, and Kitchen Bouquet®. Reduce heat to low, cover, and cook for 2 to 2 ½ hours, or until fork-tender.

Slice the meat across the grain and arrange on a platter. Spoon sauce over it and garnish with fresh parsley.

Tip: It is preferable to have a butcher cut the slit in your eye of round, as it is easy to cut your hand attempting this procedure at home.

Está en la luna de Valencia.

Someone is in the moon of Valencia.*

* Someone is in la-la land.

Salt-Dried Beef Stew ◆ Aporreado de Tasajo

The key to this traditional Cuban dish is soaking the salt-cured beef for several hours before cooking. But the residual saltiness really provides great flavor.

Serves 6 to 8

2½ pounds *tasajo* (salt-dried beef)

¼ cup olive oil

2 large onions, sliced

1 medium red bell pepper, julienne sliced

1 medium green bell pepper, julienne sliced

4 garlic cloves, minced

1 cup crushed tomatoes

1 bay leaf

1 cup low-sodium beef or chicken stock

½ cup *vino seco* (dry white cooking wine)

½ teaspoon ground cumin

½ teaspoon pepper

cooked white rice

Para atrás ni para coger impulso.

Don't step back, not even to gain momentum.

◆ At least 24 hours in advance, cut the *tasajo* in 2 to 3 pieces and place it in a large pot. Add enough cool water to cover and let the beef soak overnight.

Drain the *tasajo*, discard the water, and add enough cool water to cover. Bring the water to a boil, allow to boil 10 minutes, and discard the water. Repeat this process one more time. Add water a third time, bring to a boil, reduce heat to medium-low, cover the pot, and simmer for 1½ to 2 hours. Remove the pot from the heat and let the stock cool completely.

Remove the tasajo from the stock, cut it into 2-inch pieces, then shred the pieces. Set aside.

Heat the olive oil in a large frying pan over medium heat. Add the onions, bell peppers, and garlic and sauté for 5 to 7 minutes, until the onions are soft and translucent. Add the crushed tomatoes, bay leaf, stock, *vino seco*, cumin, and pepper, and cook for 5 minutes. Reduce the heat to low, stir in the shredded beef, and let it simmer for 45 to 50 minutes, allowing the flavors to develop fully. Remove and discard the bay leaf. Serve with white rice.

Stuffed Bell Pepper ◆ Ajíes Rellenos

This is one weekly special that goes fast at the restaurant and is one of the easiest recipes to make at home.

Serves 6

6 medium green bell peppers
1 beaten egg to bind the tops
¾ pound lean ground beef
½ pound ground pork
½ pound ground ham
2 large eggs, beaten
½ cup seasoned breadcrumbs
1 teaspoon cumin (divided)
1 teaspoon dried oregano (divided)
1 teaspoon ground black pepper
  (divided)
1 teaspoon salt, or more to taste
2 cups yellow onion, minced (divided)
6 cloves garlic, finely minced (divided)
¼ cup olive oil
2 large pimientos, diced
4 ounces crushed tomatoes
½ cup low-sodium chicken stock
cooked white rice
2 tablespoons fresh parsley

◆ Wash the green bell peppers on outside only, and cut a small circle on top of each pepper where the stem is, to remove the stem cap. Clean out the insides, and be careful not to rip them.

Beat an egg and add a pinch of salt; set aside.

Mix ground beef, pork, ham, 2 beaten eggs, and breadcrumbs with half each of the cumin, oregano, pepper, and salt. In a large skillet, cook half each of the onion and garlic in half the olive oil for 5–7 minutes, or until translucent. Remove from heat and set aside to cool.

Combine the now cooled vegetables and meat mixture. Do not overknead. Fill each bell pepper carefully with the ground beef mixture. Do not press the meat down into the pepper; rather, pack it in lightly. Brush a little of the beaten egg on the top of each pepper over the meat in order for the caps to adhere well. Cover each pepper with the corresponding cap.

Heat the remaining olive oil on medium, then sauté remaining onion, garlic, and half of the pimientos for 3 to 4 minutes. Add the tomatoes and stock and the remaining cumin and oregano. Add salt and pepper to taste. Carefully place the bell peppers standing in the sauce, spoon a little sauce over each, cover, and simmer over medium-low heat for 35 to 40 minutes. Serve with white rice and garnish with fresh parsley and the remaining pimientos.

Tip: You may also halve the peppers lengthwise and lay them flat, as they do not topple and are easier to fill. Using multicolored peppers is fun and makes the dish extra pretty.

Churrasco-Style Skirt Steak with Chimichurri Sauce
◈ Churrasco con Salsa Chimichurri

When hunger strikes, nothing satisfies like a big, juicy steak. And while our *palomilla* (minute steak) is delicious and hearty, the Churrasco-Style Steak will stick to your ribs like nobody's business. The addition of the traditional Argentinean *chimichurri* is a real treat, and any leftover sauce works well with chicken and fish.

Note: Keep the sauce tightly stored in the refrigerator for up to 5 days.

Serves 4

sea salt and fresh ground black pepper
2 skirt steaks (about 1 pound each), trimmed of fat and cut in half crosswise
1 teaspoon onion powder
1 teaspoon garlic powder

Chimichurri Sauce
4 cups flat-leaf parsley (from about 1 large bunch)
6 cloves garlic
½ to ¾ cup extra virgin olive oil
¼ cup white vinegar
salt and freshly ground black pepper
1 teaspoon red pepper flakes, optional
1 teaspoon dried oregano

◈ Rub a generous amount of salt and pepper into both sides of the steaks. Rub the onion powder and garlic powder into the steaks, dividing it evenly.

Heat a gas grill to medium-high or heat a large grill pan over medium-high heat. Grill the steaks, turning only once, to desired doneness. Remove from the grill and let rest 5 minutes. If desired, slice the steaks thinly against the grain before serving. Drizzle some of the chimichurri on the steaks and serve the rest alongside them.

For the chimichurri, pulse the parsley and garlic in a food processor until finely chopped. Scrape into a bowl and stir in the olive oil and vinegar. Season with salt and pepper, to taste. Add the red pepper flakes and the oregano.

Note: Add the pepper flakes sparingly, as they add a lot of heat.

ELLA ES

She is

UN PEDAZO

a Piece

DE PAN

of Bread.

*She is very nice.

SANDWICHES

If you show up at Versailles looking for a dry turkey sandwich on rye—hold the mayo—you are bound to get some odd looks from our waitstaff. Although they will honor your request, my guess is that they will try to convince you to indulge in any of the delicious sandwich creations on the extensive sandwich menu. If you want turkey, they might urge you to try the Elena Ruz—juicy turkey layered with cream cheese and strawberry jam in a soft *medianoche* (sweet) roll grilled to perfection. Sound better? Yeah—or how about Versailles' answer to the club sandwich, our Calle Ocho Especial? It's like a club sandwich on steroids. Crispy bacon, turkey, ham, lettuce, tomato, Swiss cheese, and mayo grilled in a sandwich press on Cuban bread—deliciously crunchy on the outside, soft and tender on the inside—and served with thin, delicately fried plantain chips. Wow, it's enough to make anyone hungry!

Of course, our Pan con Lechón is one of our most popular and most requested menu items. Why not try them and see which is your favorite? We're pretty certain that you'll love them all!

Cuban Sandwich ◈ Sandwich Cubano

A meal in itself, the Cuban Sandwich is hearty and delicious. It has been the subject of a lot of controversy and has been widely imitated and replicated. We think ours is the absolute best!

Serves 2 to 4

1 (2-foot) loaf Cuban bread
mustard
butter, at room temperature
7 ounces Swiss cheese, thinly sliced
12 ounces sweet ham, thinly sliced
7 ounces lean pork, thinly sliced
thin dill pickle slices

◈ Preheat a large frying pan or cast-iron skillet over medium-low heat or a sandwich press to 300°F.

Cut the loaf of bread in half, horizontally. Spread a thin layer of mustard evenly on one side of the bread and a thin layer of butter on the other. Layer the cheese on the bottom half of the bread, followed by the ham and pork. Layer pickles on top of the pork. Top with the top half of the bread, and press the sandwich down a little.

Cut the sandwich into the desired portions and brush the outside crusts with butter. Place the sandwiches on the preheated pan or sandwich press and press down on the sandwich with the top of the sandwich press or a heavy cast-iron pan. Cook for about 5 minutes, until the sandwich is heated through and the cheese is melted.

Tip: You may also place the sandwich open face in a toaster oven on the broiler setting to heat through.

Cuban Club Sandwich ◈ Calle Ocho Especial

You may think this is basically a club sandwich on Cuban bread, and you would be right, but everything tastes better on Cuban bread, especially with a heaping side of plantain chips!

Serves 2 to 4

1 (2-foot) loaf Cuban bread
mayonnaise
6 ounces Swiss cheese, thinly sliced
12 ounces sweet ham, thinly sliced
6 ounces turkey breast, thinly sliced
6 slices bacon, cooked until crispy
thinly sliced tomatoes
shredded lettuce
butter, at room temperature

◈ Preheat a large frying pan over medium-low heat or a sandwich press to 300°F.

Cut the loaf of bread in half, horizontally. Remove a little of the bread on the inside of one half.

Spread mayonnaise on one or both sides of the bread. Layer the cheese on the bottom half, followed by the ham and turkey. Layer the bacon on top of the turkey, then the tomato. Top with the shredded lettuce and the top half of the bread. Press the sandwich down a little.

Cut the sandwich into the desired portions and brush the outside of each sandwich with butter. Place the sandwiches on the grill and press down on the sandwich with the top of the grill or another pan. Cook for about 5 minutes, until the sandwich is heated through and the cheese is melted. Serve with mariquitas (plantain chips; see recipe, page 24).

Traime un Sandwich Cubano

I'll never forget the first time my dad brought back a Cuban sandwich and a mamey shake from the only place open late on a Saturday night, most likely from la ventanita. What was this French place called Versailles? I had never tasted something so perfectly crisp and savory and still warm in the little white paper wrapping. And this thick sweet mamey concoction perfectly balancing el sandwich cubano was nothing short of heaven.
—*Beatriz Perez*

WILL THE REAL CUBAN SANDWICH PLEASE STAND UP?

It is unbelievable that something as simple as the Cuban sandwich has caused so much controversy in the last few years.

This debate between Miami and Tampa has caused many "experts" to weigh in on the matter. Every Cuban sandwich aficionado believes in a particular version of this sandwich. In fact, they're very passionate about this and will readily argue the finer points of making our beloved Cuban sandwich with anyone who dares to challenge them.

Most Cuban sandwiches consist of sweet ham, roast pork, cheese, pickles, and a slathering of yellow ballpark mustard enclosed in a sliced length of Cuban bread and then grilled on a *plancha* (sandwich press) until crispy on the outside and warm with slightly melted cheese on the inside.

So why all the controversy? In recent years Miamians have discovered some disturbing culinary news from just a couple of hundred miles away. Apparently Tampa is trying to claim the Cuban sandwich as its own. Not so fast, Tampa; Miami isn't giving up this fight. Cuban sandwich aficionados and experts alike argue that Tampa's Cuban sandwich includes a few ingredients that are just not traditionally Cuban.

Tampa's version of the Cuban has Genoa salami and mayo! Huh? Tampa has a large Italian population as well as a large Cuban population. Could their version of the "authentic Cuban" really just be a manifestation of the melting pot that our cities have become? Perhaps, but Tampa still argues that their way is the right way.

"To the best of my knowledge there has never been salami on a Cuban sandwich, as there is no mayonnaise on a Cuban sandwich," says Raquel Roque, who has authored numerous Cuban cookbooks.

Irv Fields, the sandwich expert who operates The Café at Books & Books in Coral Gables, confirms that salami does not belong in a proper Miami Cuban sandwich. "You want a good salami sandwich, you go to a nice kosher deli. On rye bread, that's a salami sandwich," he says.

Our own Felipe Valls Jr., who serves half a million Cuban sandwiches a year, says mayo and salami would never be served on a Cuban sandwich at any of his establishments.

So who is right? Well we are, of course. But just for good measure I asked our resident star Cuban sandwich expert Joaquin from La Carreta on Bird Road in Miami. Joaquin was not too patient discussing the "Tampa sandwich," waving it off as nonsense.

Joaquin started making Cuban sandwiches in Cuba and has been doing so for more than fifty-five years. He makes as many as a hundred on any given day. That's close to two million sandwiches! He says unapologetically that the only real Cuban sandwich consists of ham, pork, Swiss or Gruyère cheese, pickles, and mustard—period, end of story. As far as we're concerned, the expert has spoken. Case closed. Sorry, Tampa.

Adapted from "Miami Engages Tampa in Cuban Sandwich War," by Hank Tester, *NBC 6 South Florida*, April 16, 2012, http://www.nbcmiami.com/news/local/Miami-Engages-Tampa-in-Cuban-Sandwich -War-147667205.html.

Versailles Special ◆ Versailles Especial

The Versailles Special is made particularly "especial" with the addition of thinly sliced chorizo. So it is a Cuban sandwich with chorizo—*not* salami. Heaven forbid! It's basically a Spanish Cuban sandwich.

Serves 2 to 4

1 (2-foot) loaf Cuban bread
mustard
7 ounces Swiss cheese, thinly sliced
12 ounces sweet ham, thinly sliced
6 slices Cantimpalo chorizo
7 ounces lean pork, thinly sliced
thin dill pickle slices
butter, at room temperature

◆ Preheat a large frying pan or cast-iron skillet over medium-low heat or a sandwich press to 300°F.

Cut the loaf of bread in half, horizontally. Remove a little of the bread on the inside of one half.

Spread a thin layer of mustard evenly on both sides of the bread. Layer the cheese on the bottom half of the bread, followed by the ham, chorizo, and pork. Layer pickles on top of the pork. Top with the top half of the bread, and press the sandwich down a little.

Cut the sandwich into the desired portions and brush the outside crusts with butter. Place the sandwiches on the preheated pan or sandwich press and press down on the sandwich with the top of the press or a heavy cast-iron pan. Cook for about 5 minutes, until the sandwich is heated through and the cheese is melted.

Elena Ruz Sandwich ◈ Elena Ruz

Who is Elena Ruz you ask, and why was a sandwich named after her? She lived in Cuba, where she frequented a restaurant called El Caramelo. She requested that her sandwich be made in this particular way so often that they put it on the menu and named it after her. This sandwich is great hot, but it is also quite good at room temperature.

Serves 1

1 ounce cream cheese, at room
   temperature
1 *medianoche* (sweet) roll
1 tablespoon strawberry preserves
3 ounces shaved turkey breast

◈ Preheat a sandwich grill or toaster oven to 350°F.

Spread the cream cheese on one slice of bread and the strawberry preserves on the other. Layer the turkey slices in between. Place the sandwich in the sandwich press or wrap it in foil and heat it in the toaster oven for 3 to 5 minutes, until heated through.

Steak Sandwich ◈ Pan con Bistec

Almost every Cuban establishment serves Pan con Bistec. There's a little variation to how it is made, but ours is traditional and really delicious.

Serves 2 to 4

3 tablespoons olive oil
¾ cup sliced onion
1½ lb. top round or sirloin steak, pounded to ¼-inch-thick *palomilla* (minute steak)
1 teaspoon onion powder
1 teaspoon garlic powder
½ teaspoon white pepper
1 teaspoon salt or more, to taste
1 (2-foot) loaf Cuban bread, split horizontally
potato sticks
ketchup (optional)
shredded lettuce
sliced tomatoes

◈ Heat the olive oil in a cast-iron skillet over medium-high heat. Add the onion and sauté for 5 to 7 minutes, until soft. Transfer the onion to a plate and reheat the skillet.

Season the steak generously with onion powder, garlic powder, pepper, and salt. Add it to the hot skillet and fry it for 1 to 2 minutes per side, until it is cooked to the desired doneness.

Place the steak on the bottom half of the bread and top with the sautéed onions and any pan drippings. Top with a mound of potato sticks, ketchup (if desired), lettuce, tomatoes, and the other half of the bread. Cut into desired portions and serve immediately.

Midnight Sandwich ◆ Medianoche

The Medianoche earned its name because it was usually served at or after midnight at Havana nightclubs. Our Medianoche is very similar to a Cuban Sandwich. The only real difference is the bread that is used to make it. We use a soft egg bread that is long, like a hoagie, and a little sweet. These can be found at Hispanic markets or Cuban bakeries. At regular supermarkets, look for a long roll (think hot dog bun, but wider) that is a little shiny on top.

Serves 1

1 (6-inch) *medianoche* roll or other
   sweet, eggy roll
mustard
2 to 4 slices dill pickle
2 ounces Swiss cheese, thinly sliced
2 to 3 ounces sweet ham, thinly sliced
1 to 2 ounces roast pork, thinly sliced
butter, at room temperature

◆ Preheat a large frying pan over medium-low heat or a sandwich press to 300°F.

Cut the roll in half horizontally and lightly spread mustard on each side. On the bottom half of the bread layer the ham, pork, cheese, and pickles, and add the top half of the bread.

Brush the outside of the sandwich with butter, then place it on the sandwich press or preheated skillet and press down with the top of the press or a heavy cast-iron pan. Cook for about 5 minutes, until the sandwich is heated through and the cheese is melted.

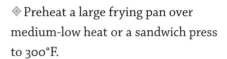

Going to Get Abuelo

I grew up right around the corner. I remember going on my bike to fetch my abuelo for dinner. Always talking politics and stuff on the corner. Sometimes they would get very heated. Great memories.
—Bryant Herrera

Croquette Sandwich with Ham and Cheese ◈ Croqueta Preparada

This famous sandwich is a Cuban Sandwich with two ham croquettes added before pressing it down in a sandwich grill.

Serves 2 to 4

1 (2-foot) loaf Cuban bread
7 ounces Swiss cheese, thinly sliced
12 ounces sweet ham, thinly sliced
8 fried ham croquettes (approximately 2 per sandwich)
2 to 4 slices dill pickle
butter, at room temperature

◈ Preheat a large frying pan or cast-iron skillet over medium-low heat or a sandwich press to 300°F.

Cut the loaf of bread in half, horizontally. Remove a little of the bread on the inside of one half.

On the bottom half of the bread, layer the cheese, ham, croquettes, and pickles and top with the other half of the bread. Press the sandwich down a little.

Cut the sandwich into the desired portions and brush the outside crusts with butter. Place the sandwiches on the preheated pan or sandwich press and press down on the sandwich with the top of the press or a heavy cast-iron pan. Cook for about 5 minutes, until the sandwich is heated through and the cheese is melted.

Roast Pork Sandwich ◈ Pan con Lechón

We're pretty sure Pan con Lechón was invented because Cubans never knew what to do with leftover pork after we roast those whole pigs. What better way to enjoy leftovers. Don't forget the *mojo*!

Serves 2 to 4

1 (2-foot) loaf Cuban bread, cut in half horizontally
½ cup Mojo Criollo (see recipe, page 21)
1½ pounds roast pork, heated
1 cup thinly sliced cooked onion

◈ Place the bread in a warm oven for a few minutes just to heat it through (not toast it). Spread mojo criollo on each side of the bread. Add the pork, then the onion, and the top half of the bread. Cut into desired portions and serve immediately.

Chicken Sandwich ◈ Sandwich de Pechuga de Pollo

This is our delicious chicken breast sandwich that everyone seems to love.

Serves 2 to 4

1 tablespoon garlic powder
1 tablespoon onion powder
1 teaspoon salt
½ teaspoon white pepper
4 boneless, skinless chicken breasts,
   pounded to ¼-inch thickness
¼ cup olive oil
1 loaf fresh Cuban bread
2 tablespoons mayonnaise
8 thin slices of tomato
shredded iceberg lettuce

◈ Combine the garlic powder, onion powder, salt, and pepper in a small bowl. Arrange the chicken breasts on a plate, season them generously with the spice mixture, and set aside. Cover the dish with plastic wrap and set the chicken aside at room temperature for 30 minutes.

Heat the olive oil in a large frying pan over medium-high heat. Add the chicken to the hot oil and cook for 5 minutes on each side, or until golden brown.

Cut the Cuban loaf in 4 pieces and place a chicken breast on the bottom half of each. Spread mayonnaise on the other side of the bread, and top the chicken with thinly sliced tomato and shredded iceberg lettuce and the other half of the bread.

Fish Sandwich ◈ Sandwich de Pescado

This fresh fish sandwich with tangy tartar sauce on Cuban bread hits the spot every time!

Serves 2 to 4

1 loaf fresh Cuban bread
4 6-ounce mahimahi fillets
¼ cup prepared tartar sauce
8 iceberg lettuce leaves
4 slices vine-ripened tomato
2 teaspoons garlic powder
2 teaspoons onion powder
2 teaspoons salt
1 teaspoon white pepper

◈ In a large nonstick skillet heat butter over medium-high heat. Season mahi-mahi fillets with garlic powder, onion powder, and salt and pepper. Cook for 3 to 4 minutes per side until fish flakes easily. Slice Cuban bread and toast lightly. Assemble sandwich by spreading tartar sauce on both pieces of bread, with the mahimahi fillet topped with lettuce and tomatoes in between.

This will
SE ACABÓ
finish like
COMO LA FIESTA
Guatao's
DEL GUATAO.
party.*

*This is going to
end badly.

SIDE DISHES AND SNACKS

When ordering lunch or dinner at Versailles, you have the option of two sides or *acompañantes*. These not-so-little side dishes are the source of a lot of angst. There are so many to choose from. The combinations are endless, thereby making each meal at Versailles a brand new experience.

These side dishes really don't need a main course to make them special. Guests create entire meals from side dishes alone. These sidekick side dishes really are the heart and soul of our Cuban heritage. So, when picking out a menu, be sure to include at least two and preferably three or four of these special dishes to make your Cuban meal extra special.

We probably should have called this chapter "plantains and more plantains." We certainly love them, and they are among the best-selling items on our menu. Because the plantain is so versatile, we had to include several of our most popular recipes in this chapter. These and our other favorite side dishes complement our savory and delectable main courses perfectly.

Corn Tamales

These tamales are really popular both as an appetizer and as a main course. They go particularly well with our delicious *croquetas*.

Makes 12 to 16 tamales

1½ pounds pork in small chunks (about 1½- to 2-inch pieces)

2 cloves garlic, whole, peeled

1 tablespoon white vinegar

3 cups ground fresh or frozen yellow corn kernels

¾ cup salted butter

2½ cups yellow cornmeal

½ teaspoon bijol (yellow coloring)

3 cups low-sodium chicken stock, divided (2½ cups and ½ cup)

¼ cup olive oil for frying

1 large onion, chopped fine

1 large green pepper, finely diced

4 cloves garlic, minced

3 tablespoons tomato paste

½ cup *vino seco* (dry white cooking wine)

¼ cup lime juice

1 teaspoon salt or more to taste

½ teaspoon white pepper

24–32 dried cornhusks (soak dried cornhusks in hot water before using)

◈ Season pork chunks with salt and place in a medium pot. Add just enough water to cover the meat and add the garlic cloves and vinegar. Bring to a boil. Reduce heat to low to medium-low and cook uncovered until all the water has evaporated. Allow the pork chunks to fry in the rendered fat just until light golden brown. Do not cook too long; the meat should be tender but not crispy.

Drain the pork on paper towels, chop into very small pieces, and set aside.

Place the corn in a food processor with the butter and pulse several times, just enough to get a coarse mixture. Place in a large pot, add yellow cornmeal and bijol, and mix well. Add 2½ cups of stock, stir, and set aside.

In another skillet, heat the olive oil over medium heat. Add the onion and green pepper and cook, stirring occasionally, until the onions are soft and translucent. Add the garlic and continue cooking for an additional 3 minutes. Heat ½ cup of the stock and combine it with the tomato paste. Add this to the onion mixture followed by the wine and the lime juice. Stir well and continue cooking over medium heat for 10 to 15 minutes.

Add the pork and the onion mixture to the pot with the yellow cornmeal. Season with salt and pepper to taste and cook over low heat, stirring frequently, until the mixture thickens, around 20 to 25 minutes, adding more stock if necessary. The mixture should be stiff, but stirring it should not be difficult. Remove from heat and allow to cool.

To make the tamales, place two cornhusks on a large, flat working surface and overlap them halfway from end to end. Place about ⅓ cup of the corn and pork mixture in the center of the cornhusks. Fold the short sides of the cornhusks in and then the two long ends over each other. Secure in the center with kitchen string.

You may use a tamale steamer or a large stockpot to cook these. Fill the stockpot with about 2 inches of water. Stand the tamales on end and leaning against the side of the pot. Bring the water to a boil, reduce heat to low, and cook covered for about 1½ to 2 hours. These may be enjoyed hot or at room temperature. It is best to refrigerate the tamales for several hours or overnight and reheat just before eating.

Tip: These heat very well in the microwave.

Fried Sweet Plantains ◈ Platanitos Maduros

A highly popular side dish, these can usually be found on the side of any Cuban plate. Since we love our sweet and salty combination, we believe that *maduros* taste great with anything! Look for dark-skinned really ripe plantains for this recipe. Ripeness makes all the difference. The riper the plantain, the more caramelization you will have around the edges of the maduros.

Serves 4 to 6

2 to 3 cups corn or vegetable oil
2 or 3 large *very ripe* (black) plantains

◈ Heat 2 to 3 inches of oil to 375°F in a large, heavy pot over medium-high heat.

Peel the plantains as you would a banana. Because they are soft, the skin will come off easily. Slice the plantains diagonally into 1-inch pieces. Carefully place 4 or 5 plantain slices into the hot oil and cook, turning only once, for about 2 to 3 minutes on each side, until golden brown. Transfer the fried plantains to a paper towel–lined plate to drain, and continue with the remaining plantains. Serve immediately.

Fried Green Plantains ◈ Tostones

Tostones are another variation on the fried plantain theme. Here, green plantains are fried, then flattened, then fried again. Use really dark green plantains, peel them, and soak them in salted water for ten to fifteen minutes before frying them. Be sure to dry the plantains well before frying them, to prevent the hot oil from splattering.

Serves 6 to 8

3 cups corn oil
3 Hawaiian plantains or green plantains
coarse salt

◈ Heat 2 to 3 inches of oil to 375°F in a large, heavy pot over medium heat.

Cut about half an inch from both ends of each plantain, then cut each plantain, with the skin on, into 1½- to 2-inch slices. Use your knife to peel the skin off each slice.

Carefully place 4 or 5 plantain slices in the oil; it should be hot enough to bubble around the plantain, but not so vigorously that it begins to add color right away. Fry the plantains for 3 minutes on each side, then transfer them to a paper towel–lined plate to drain and cool slightly. Fry the remaining slices in the same manner, allowing the oil to return to 375°F between batches. Leave the oil over medium-low heat for the second stage of frying.

Once you have fried all of the slices, start flattening them, beginning with the first batch, which should have cooled by now. Place the plantain slices, one at a time, between two pieces of wax or parchment paper and press down with the heel of your hand, flattening the plantain slices to about ¾-inch thickness. Continue with the remaining slices.

Fry the plantains a second time, in batches, for about 2 to 3 minutes on each side, until they are golden and crispy around the edges. Transfer them to a paper towel–lined plate to drain and sprinkle them generously with coarse salt. Serve immediately.

Mixed Black Beans and Rice Dish ◈ Moros

This is a Cuban classic. It is black beans and rice mixed into one delectable dish, the perfect accompaniment to almost anything.

Serves 6 to 8

½ pound dried black beans, rinsed
1 teaspoon salt, plus more as needed
1 bay leaf
¼ cup plus 2 tablespoons olive oil
¼ pound bacon
1 green bell pepper, chopped
2 medium onions, chopped

3 garlic cloves, minced
1 pound converted white rice
¼ cup *vino seco* (dry white cooking wine)
1 teaspoon dried oregano
½ teaspoon ground cumin
½ teaspoon black pepper

◈ In a large pot bring 6 cups of water to a boil over medium-high heat. Add the beans, salt, and bay leaf, reduce the heat to low, cover the pot, and let the beans simmer for about 2 hours, or until they are fork-tender.

Let the beans cool to room temperature then drain them, reserving 3 cups of their cooking liquid. Remove and discard the bay leaf. Set aside.

Heat 2 tablespoons of the olive oil in the same pot over medium-high heat. Cook the bacon until it is crispy and renders most of its fat. Discard half the fat, then add 2 tablespoons of the olive oil, the bell pepper, onions, and garlic, and sauté for 5 to 7 minutes, until the vegetables are soft and caramelized. Add the rice, the 3 cups reserved bean liquid, *vino seco*, oregano, cumin, and pepper, and bring to a boil; boil for 5 minutes.

Meanwhile, combine the beans with the remaining 2 tablespoons of olive oil and season with salt to taste. Add to the rice mixture and continue boiling, uncovered, for 10 minutes, until most of the water is absorbed by the rice. Reduce the heat to low, cover the pot, and let the beans and rice simmer for an additional 15 to 20 minutes, until all the liquid is absorbed. Fluff the rice with a fork, taste, and adjust the seasonings, if necessary.

Tip: Always look for beans that are uniform in size and color. When selecting black beans, the deeper the color of the bean, the richer the final product will taste. Dry beans can also be cooked quickly with a pressure cooker—just follow the manufacturer's directions.

White Rice ◈ Arroz Blanco

White rice is a simple side dish, but it is the perfect base for so many of our rich, hearty dishes and a must with our black beans.

Serves 4

1½ teaspoons salt
1 cup long grain white rice (we like Mahatma® brand)
2 tablespoons vegetable, corn, or canola oil

Note: Most Cubans wash their rice or at least rinse it quickly under cold water before cooking it. We now know that rinsing rice eliminates some vitamins and nutrients. But traditionalists still rinse their rice because that's how it was done in Cuba.

◈ Bring 2 cups cold water to a boil in a medium-sized saucepan. Add the salt, rice, and oil. Continue boiling for 2 minutes. Reduce heat to low, stir the rice, cover the pan, and let the rice simmer for 20 to 25 minutes, until almost all the liquid has been soaked up by the rice. Remove the pan from the heat, fluff the rice with a fork, and add more salt, if necessary.

Mashed Plantains ◆ Fufu de Plátano

Fufu has the most unique flavor and texture of almost any Cuban dish. It is very comforting, like mashed potatoes, but substantially heartier and more savory.

Serves 4 to 6

3 green plantains, cut into 2-inch slices
1 ripe plantain, cut into 2-inch slices
2 pounds pork chops, cubed
⅓ cup olive oil
1 medium onion, chopped
3 garlic cloves, minced
1 medium red bell pepper, chopped
½ cup milk
½ teaspoon sweet paprika
½ teaspoon salt, plus more to season pork
½ teaspoon pepper, plus more to season pork

◆ Fill a large pot with water, add the plantain slices, and bring to a boil. Let the plantains boil for 40 to 45 minutes, until tender. Drain and peel the plantains and set them aside.

Season the pork chops generously with salt and pepper. Heat the olive oil in a large frying pan over medium-high heat. Add the pork and cook for about 5 to 7 minutes, until crispy. Add the onion, garlic, and bell pepper, and reduce the heat to medium. Cook for 5 to 7 minutes, until the onion is translucent. Add the plantains and mash them into the onion/pork mixture with the back of a wooden spoon or a large fork. Add about half of the milk, the paprika, salt, and pepper, and continue mashing and stirring. Add more milk until desired consistency is achieved. Taste and adjust the seasonings, if necessary. Serve immediately.

Versailles: "The After Party!"

I can't remember a prom, gala, event, or party that didn't end at Versailles! I will always remember the words we all said as teenagers: "Pa Versailles? I'm starving." And there we all were in our suits, sequins, big dresses, some of the girls in flip flops from the achy feet, just looking forward to the croquettes, café con leche, tostadas among many delicious goodies in the wee hours of the night!
—*Vicky del Pino*

Yellow Rice ◈ Arroz Amarillo

Many of our patrons prefer yellow rice with our black beans. But it is also delicious on its own or as part of a recipe like our Paella Versailles.

Serves 6 to 8

¼ cup olive oil
1 large onion, finely chopped
1 medium green bell pepper, minced
3 garlic cloves, minced
½ cup crushed tomatoes
1 bay leaf
2 cups converted white rice
1 cup short grain or Valencia rice
1½ teaspoons bijol (yellow coloring)
½ teaspoon dried oregano
½ teaspoon ground cumin
½ teaspoon black pepper
4 cups low-sodium chicken stock
salt to taste (be sure to taste before adding salt, as the stock adds a lot of salt)

◈ In a large pot, heat olive oil over medium heat. Cook onions and bell pepper for 5 to 7 minutes, until translucent. Add garlic and cook for another 3 minutes. Add crushed tomatoes and bay leaf and cook 3 minutes more.

Add the rice and stir well to combine. Add the bijol and the remaining spices. Add the stock and stir well. Bring to a boil. Allow to cook uncovered for 2 minutes. Reduce heat to low, cover, and continue cooking for 20 to 25 minutes until all liquid is absorbed and rice is tender.

Yuca with Garlic Sauce ◈ Yuca con Mojo Criollo

Yuca is a unique and mildly flavored root vegetable that stands up very well to the tangy, savory *mojo*, or garlic sauce. The Versailles recipe calls for fresh yuca. However, it is a rare vegetable not often readily available in markets, and frozen yuca is a great alternative.

Serves 4

3 large or 4 medium yuca (about 2 pounds), peeled and cut into 3-inch chunks, or 1 (2.5-pound) bag frozen yuca
salt
Mojo Criollo (see recipe, page 21)

◈ To make the yuca, fill a large pot with water, add the yuca and salt to taste, and bring to a boil. Boil, uncovered, for 5 minutes, then reduce the heat to medium-low and cover. Cook for 1 hour to 1 hour and 15 minutes, until the yuca is fork-tender.

Drain the yuca and serve it hot, with mojo criollo.

EL HORNO

The oven's

NO ESTÁ PARA

not ready for

GALLETICAS.

cookies.*

*Don't push your luck.

Desserts

Cubans are notorious for having an almost insatiable sweet tooth. In fact, it was that need to satisfy our most intense cravings that persuaded us to open Versailles Bakery. Our Pastelitos de Guayaba (guava pastries) are now famous after being featured on the Food Network's *Best Thing I Ever Ate*. Nothing beats the aroma and mouth-watering taste of a freshly baked *pastelito*.

But our desserts are varied and notoriously delicious. We're including just a sampling of our most popular ones. For a really authentic Cuban breakfast experience, head on over to our bakery on a Sunday morning; order a *cortadito*, a guava *pastelito*, a meat *pastelito*, and a *croqueta de jamón*—then grab a copy of *El Nuevo Herald* and immerse yourself in our Cuban culture and flavors.

It is impossible not to salivate upon entering the bakery at Versailles. The aroma, the visual appeal, and the incomparable flavors make you want to stay there forever. We often joke that no respectable Cuban can get up from the dinner table without dessert. We are genetically coded to love sweets. Perhaps it has something to do with all the sugarcane fields in Cuba. As you can imagine, dessert is very important in our culture, and delectable treats like the ones in this chapter are sure to please any crowd.

Cuban Flan ◇ Flan Cubano

Flan is probably the most common of all Cuban desserts. The coconut-flavored variation is a favorite at Versailles.

Serves 6

¾ cup sugar
4 large whole eggs
2 large egg yolks
1 (14-ounce) can condensed milk
1 (14-ounce) can evaporated milk
1 teaspoon vanilla extract
¼ teaspoon salt

For Coconut Flan
1 can shredded coconut in heavy
    syrup, drained, with half of the syrup
    reserved

◇ Preheat the oven to 325°F.

Heat ½ cup of the sugar in a small saucepan over medium-low heat,

stirring occasionally, for 5 to 7 minutes, until the sugar melts. Watch it closely so that it does not burn. Once the sugar has completely melted and turned a light caramel color, pour it evenly into six 4- to 6-ounce ramekins.

Combine the remaining sugar, eggs, egg yolks, condensed milk, evaporated milk, vanilla, and salt in a blender and blend until completely combined, then pour the mixture into the ramekins.

Fill a large rectangular baking pan halfway with water. Carefully set the ramekins in the water (baño de María), and place the pan on the center rack of the oven. Bake for about 40 to 50 minutes, until the centers of the custards are set.

Remove the ramekins from the water-filled pan and let them cool to room temperature. Refrigerate for at least 4 hours.

Before serving, run a knife around the sides of the ramekins to loosen the flan.

You can also dip the bottom halves of the ramekins in some warm (not hot) water for about 30 seconds to ensure that the bottom of the flan releases with ease. Invert the cups onto small plates.

For Coconut Flan variation: Top each flan with the shredded coconut and syrup. To serve, place a dollop of the coconut mixture next to each flan.

Cheese Flan ◈ Flan de Queso

This is a cross between a Cuban flan and a traditional cheesecake. It's a wonderful mix, making a denser, richer flan.

Serves 6

1 cup sugar
4 large whole eggs
2 large egg yolks
1 (14-ounce) can condensed milk
1 (14-ounce) can evaporated milk
1 teaspoon vanilla extract
8 ounces cream cheese, at room
  temperature
¼ teaspoon salt

◈ Preheat the oven to 325°F.

Heat ½ cup of the sugar in a small saucepan over medium-low heat, stirring occasionally, for 15 to 20 minutes, until the sugar melts. Watch it closely so that it does not burn. Once the sugar has completely melted and turned a light caramel color, pour it evenly into six 4- to 6-ounce ramekins.

Combine the remaining sugar, eggs, egg yolks, condensed milk, evaporated milk, vanilla, cream cheese, and salt in a blender and blend until completely combined. Pour evenly into the ramekins.

Fill a large rectangular baking pan halfway with water. Carefully place the ramekins into the water in the pan (baño de María), and place the pan on the center rack of the oven. Bake for about 40 to 50 minutes, until the centers of the custards are set.

Take the ramekins out of the water and let them cool to room temperature. Refrigerate for at least 4 hours.

Before serving, run a knife around the sides of the ramekins to loosen the flan. You can also dip the bottom halves of the ramekins in warm (not hot) water for about 30 seconds to ensure that the bottom of the flan releases with ease. Invert the cups onto small plates.

Vanilla Custard ◈ Natilla Versailles

Natilla is basically Cuban *crème brûlée* or a rich vanilla pudding. Most places serve traditional *natilla* with a light sprinkling of cinnamon, which is how it is done at Versailles. You can also caramelize the top with a little kitchen torch for a special presentation of this classic.

Serves 8

4 cups whole milk
8 large egg yolks
1½ cups sugar
¼ teaspoon salt
¼ cup cornstarch
2 teaspoons pure vanilla extract
ground cinnamon, for sprinkling

◈ Combine the milk, egg yolks, sugar, salt, and cornstarch in a large bowl. Stir well, until the sugar is completely dissolved. Strain the mixture through a fine sieve into a heavy saucepan. Stir in the vanilla and set the pan over medium heat. Cook the mixture, stirring continuously with a whisk or wooden spoon until it begins to boil, then reduce the heat to medium-low and cook until the mixture thickens, for 15 to 20 minutes.

Pour the custard into individual ramekins and set aside to cool to room temperature. Cover the ramekins lightly with plastic wrap and refrigerate for at least 1 hour, until the custard sets. Sprinkle with cinnamon immediately before serving.

From Marlins Park to Versailles

I went to a Marlins game at the new Marlins park with my family, including my aunt and uncle, who are in their early nineties. They were caught by the kiss cam and didn't realize it, so the camera kept going back to them to get them to kiss on camera. Finally after about three or four times, they realized that they were on camera and were being asked to kiss. My aunt kept trying to grab my uncle's face to kiss him, but he continued to refuse to do it on camera. Everyone at the stadium would cheer them on to kiss and laugh when my uncle rejected my aunt. Again, the camera kept going back to them throughout the game, and finally, just before the game ended, they kissed on camera!

After the game we usually go to Versailles, and when we walked in almost everyone at the restaurant recognized my aunt and uncle from the game. All of a sudden they were famous! Diners wanted to come up to them and greet them while we ate our dinner. We were even approached by Oscar Haza from A Mano Limpia! It was surely a day we will never forget.
—Jessica Rodriguez

Three Milks ◈ Tres Leches

Originally a Nicaraguan delicacy but adapted to Cuban palates, this super-sweet and rich dessert is a best seller. Although it is a little time-consuming to make, it is well worth the effort.

Serves 8

Cake

6 large eggs, separated
1½ cups granulated sugar
½ cup whole milk
2 teaspoons vanilla extract
2 cups all-purpose flour
2 teaspoons baking powder

Filling

1 (14-ounce) can evaporated milk
1 (14-ounce) can sweetened condensed milk
1 cup heavy cream
2 tablespoons white rum (optional)

Cuban-Style Meringue

3 tablespoons water
¾ cup granulated sugar
3 large egg whites
Maraschino cherries, as garnish (optional)

◈ Preheat the oven to 350° F. Lightly grease and flour a 9 by 13–inch baking dish and set aside.

In a large bowl, beat the egg whites on medium until soft peaks form. Gradually add the sugar. Add the egg yolks, beating well after each yolk. Combine the milk and vanilla and set aside. Sift flour and baking powder and add to the egg mixture, alternating with adding the milk and vanilla to the egg mixture.

Pour into baking dish and bake until golden, about 25 to 30 minutes.

For the filling, whisk together the evaporated milk, condensed milk, and heavy cream. Remove the cake from the oven and pour the milk mixture over it while still warm. Allow it to come to room temperature before refrigerating it for at least 4 hours or overnight.

For the meringue, in a heavy saucepan combine the water and sugar and bring it to a boil. Reduce the heat and stir to dissolve the sugar. Continue boiling until the mixture reaches the soft ball stage (240°F) and remove from the heat.

Beat the egg whites until soft peaks form. Begin to add the syrup in a steady stream while beating until all the syrup has been added and the meringue is glossy. Spread the meringue over the chilled cake and decorate with maraschino cherries before serving each portion.

Bread Pudding ◈ Pudín de Pan

Cuban bread pudding is a little different from the bread pudding that is so in vogue these days. Ours is served chilled and topped with simple syrup.

Serves 8

1 cup whole milk

1 (14-ounce) can sweetened condensed milk

1 (14-ounce) can light fruit cocktail, undrained

1 teaspoon vanilla extract

½ teaspoon ground cinnamon

½ cup light brown sugar

¼ cup sliced almonds, lightly toasted

¼ chopped pecans

¼ cup dried apricots, chopped

¼ cup raisins

3 tablespoons brandy or amaretto

4 large eggs, beaten

pinch salt

1 (2-foot) loaf day-old Cuban bread, torn into 2-inch pieces

6 tablespoons salted butter, melted

Tip: If you can't get Cuban bread, you may substitute day-old French bread.

◈ Preheat the oven to 350°F.

Combine the milk, condensed milk, fruit cocktail, vanilla, cinnamon, brown sugar, almonds, pecans, apricots, raisins, brandy, eggs, and salt in a large bowl and mix well.

In another large bowl, toss the bread with 4 tablespoons of the melted butter. Use the remaining 2 tablespoons of melted butter to grease a 2-quart glass baking dish.

Pour the milk mixture over the bread and toss well. Allow this mixture to sit for 35 to 45 minutes, until most of the liquid is absorbed by the bread. Pour the bread mixture into the prepared baking pan and bake for 1 to 1½ hours, until the pudding sets.

Serve warm or set aside to cool to room temperature, then refrigerate for 4 hours or overnight. Top with simple syrup.

Simple Syrup

1 cup sugar

1 cup water

zest from half a lime

1 stick cinnamon

pinch salt

Combine all the ingredients in a small saucepan and bring the mixture to a boil. Reduce the heat to low and cook until the mixture reduces by half, about 15 to 20 minutes. Remove the cinnamon and lime zest (strain if desired) and chill before serving.

Rice Pudding ◈ Arroz con Leche

This rice pudding is creamy and dense, and everyone loves our special version. It's really delicious hot from the pot too.

Serves 8

¾ cup short grain white rice
   (Valencia or Italian arborio rice)
1 tablespoon butter
rind of half a lime
2 cups whole milk
1 (14-ounce) can sweetened
   condensed milk
½ cup sugar
1 cinnamon stick
¼ teaspoon salt
ground cinnamon

◈ Bring 2 cups of water to boil in a heavy saucepan over medium-high heat. Add the rice and butter and cook, uncovered, for 5 minutes. Reduce the heat to low, cover the pan, and continue cooking for another 20 minutes. Remove from the heat and set aside.

Using a vegetable peeler, carefully peel away the lime rind, green part only, from the lime. You will be removing this from the pudding later on, so make sure you leave this in larger peelings.

In a large bowl, combine the lime rind, milk, condensed milk, sugar, cinnamon stick, and salt.

Use a fork to fluff up the rice, making sure it is not stuck to the bottom of the pot. Add the milk mixture and return the pan to the stove. Cook over low heat, stirring frequently, for 40 to 45 minutes, until the pudding thickens. Set aside to cool to room temperature, then refrigerate for at least 1 hour, until the pudding sets.

To serve, remove the cinnamon stick and lime rind and sprinkle with a generous amount of cinnamon.

Guava and Cream Cheese Pie ◈ Pastel de Guayaba y Queso

Don't confuse the guava pie with guava *pastelitos* (pastries). This is an actual pie. Delicious warm and à la mode!

Serves 8

2 refrigerated pie crusts

8 ounces cream cheese, in thin slices (approximately ¼-inch thick)

8 ounces guava paste, in thin slices (approximately ¼-inch thick)

3 ounces guava shells, drained from their syrup, cut in half

1 egg, beaten with 1 tablespoon of water

◈ Preheat oven to 400°F. Spray a 9-inch pie plate with nonstick baking spray.

Place one of the refrigerated pie crusts on the plate and press lightly. Poke several holes in the bottom pie crust with the tines of a fork to allow the steam to escape while baking. Place in the preheated oven for 5 minutes.

Remove from oven and allow to cool. Reduce oven temperature to 325°F.

Alternate slices of the cream cheese and guava uniformly inside the pie crust. Place the guava shells along the inside border of the pie pan. Place the other pie crust on top of the now filled crust and seal the edges with a decorative scallop design or by crimping the edges with a fork. With a sharp knife make several small slits on the top of the crust. (You may also do a lattice design with the top crust). Brush the top of the pie with the beaten egg mixture. Bake in a 325°F oven for 40 to 45 minutes, or until the crust is a light golden brown. May be served warm or at room temperature.

Plenty of Room for Dessert!

My mom and I had lunch one day at Versailles. When it came time for dessert, the waiter came and asked if we were interested. Having had a sweet tooth all my life and knowing of the delectable and perfectly wonderful desserts here, I gladly and wholeheartedly ordered the flan de mamey. The waiter then turned to my mom and said, "And you, madam?" My mom gave her usual response: that she would just eat from her daughter's.

I responded rather loudly, "No waaay! I will not share my dessert with anyone. Bring her her own flan de mamey." My mom said she was not hungry enough to eat the whole thing. I said not to worry—I'd just eat what she left behind.

That was when I noticed the giggles and smiles of the fellow patrons and the waiter.
—*Margaret Sanchez*

Guava Cheesecake ◆ Cheesecake de Guayaba

Guava and cream cheese are a match made in heaven and a classic Cuban combination! Naturally Versailles' Guava Cheesecake is a hit among its patrons.

Serves 8 to 10

4 tablespoons salted butter, at room temperature

1½ cups graham cracker crumbs

1 cup sugar

16 ounces cream cheese, at room temperature

1 tablespoon vanilla extract

½ cup half and half

2 egg yolks

4 whole eggs

1 cup guava marmalade

◆ Preheat the oven to 400°F.

Combine the butter, graham cracker crumbs, and ¼ cup of the sugar in a bowl. Firmly press this mixture into the bottom and about 1 inch up the sides of an 8- or 9-inch springform pan. Place the pan on a baking sheet and bake for 10 minutes. Set aside to cool. Leave the oven set to 400°F.

In a large bowl, beat the cream cheese, vanilla, and remaining ¾ cup sugar with an electric mixer until fluffy. Gradually add the half and half and mix until the mixture is thin and free of lumps. Add the egg yolks and then the eggs one at a time until combined. Pour the mixture into the cooled pie crust and bake for 15 minutes at 400°F. Reduce the heat to 300°F and bake for 1 hour and 15 minutes more. Turn off the heat and allow the cheesecake to cool in the oven with the oven door partially open.

Once the cheesecake has reached room temperature, cover it with plastic wrap and refrigerate for at least 6 hours, preferably overnight.

Spread the cup of guava marmalade over the top of the cheesecake before serving.

Note: You may also top with guava shells.

Cuban-Style French Toast ◆ Torrejas

Torrejas is the Spanish and Cuban version of French toast. However, it is sweeter and more decadent than classic French toast, and Versailles serves it as dessert as well as for breakfast.

Serves 6 to 8

4 eggs, beaten
1 (14-ounce) can evaporated milk
1 cup sugar
2 teaspoons *vino seco* (dry white
   cooking wine)
1 teaspoon vanilla extract
1 teaspoon ground cinnamon
1 loaf Cuban bread
2 cups vegetable oil for frying

◆ Mix eggs, milk, sugar, wine, vanilla, and cinnamon; cut bread in slices less than 1 inch thick. Soak bread in the milk mixture. Fry in hot oil until lightly golden. Serve with simple syrup (see recipe, page 152) or maple syrup.

Sweet Caramel Milk Curds ◆ Dulce de Leche Cortada

A classic and addictive Cuban treat.

Serves 8 to 10

2 gallons milk
12 pieces lemon rind (use 2 or 3 lemons
   and avoid including too much pith,
   which is bitter)
5 eggs
2½ cups sugar
½ teaspoon salt

◆ Divide the milk among four 2-quart containers. Put 3 pieces of lemon rind in each container. Allow the milk to sit undisturbed in your refrigerator for 2 to 3 days, until it curdles.

In a large pot bring the curdled milk to a boil over medium heat. Reduce heat to low and simmer uncovered for 1 hour.

Remove 1 cup of liquid from the pot (leaving the curd behind). Put 5 eggs in a blender and blend at medium-high speed. Very slowly, add the hot liquid that was removed from the pot in a thin, steady stream to the eggs. Blend until the eggs are frothy. Add the egg mixture, little by little, into the simmering milk curds, stirring constantly until well blended. After 2 hours, add the sugar and the salt. Continue simmering over very low heat, stirring frequently, until almost all the liquid has evaporated. This may take another 2 hours. Be sure to stir frequently and keep the temperature low to avoid burning.

Remove from heat and allow to cool completely before refrigerating. Serve on its own in small bowls or martini glasses.

Heavenly Custard ◈ Tocinillo del Cielo

Tocinillo del Cielo is a well-known Cuban dessert that became really popular after President Bill Clinton ordered it at our restaurant. Who can blame him? It is richer than a flan because it's sweeter and made with egg yolks. Give it a try—you may agree with the president!

Serves 8

3 cups white sugar
2 cups water
peel of 1 medium orange
1 cinnamon stick
12 egg yolks
2 teaspoons pure vanilla extract

◈ Preheat oven to 350°F. Use a soufflé or a baking dish with about 5-cup capacity. (You can also use individual ovenproof custard cups.)

For the caramel that goes into the baking dish or cups first, heat 1 cup of the sugar in the bottom of a metallic pan at medium-high heat until it begins to melt. Stir constantly to prevent burning. The sugar will turn to a thick syrup with a light brown color. Quickly remove from heat and pour into your flan dish or into individual custard cups. Tilt back and forth to cover the bottom and sides of the dish. The syrup will harden as it cools, to form a thick shell. During the baking process this shell magically transforms itself into a delicious dark caramel syrup.

For the body of the tocinillo, combine the remaining 2 cups of sugar with the water in a 3-quart saucepan. Add the orange peel and cinnamon and boil at high heat, stirring occasionally, until the syrup reaches a temperature of 220°F. Remove from heat and let cool until warm. Remove orange peel and cinnamon stick.

Beat egg yolks by hand with a whisk. Gradually add cooled (slightly warm) syrup and vanilla. Blend to a smooth consistency, but don't overwhip.

After all the ingredients are combined, place the mixture in the caramelized baking dish or individual custard cups.

Next, fill a large rectangular baking pan halfway with water. Carefully place the baking dish or ramekins into the water in the pan (baño de María) and place the pan on the center rack of the oven. Bake in the oven for 45 minutes to 1 hour. To check for doneness, test with a toothpick or fork while baking; the tester should come out relatively clean.

After the tocinillo is fully cooked, set aside and let cool. Place in the refrigerator for about 3 hours. When ready to serve, run a knife along the edge to loosen it. Place a serving platter over the bowl or cups and flip quickly. Make sure to scrape any caramel residue from the bowl or cups onto the tocinillo.

You
TU NO MOJAS,
don't wet,
PERO EMPAPAS.
you drench.

Beverages

The beverages at Versailles are numerous and vary from traditional sweet sodas like Materva®, Ironbeer®, and Jupiña® to fruit and puffed wheat shakes to accompany your savory dishes and delight your palate. If you need something a little stronger, our mojitos hit the mark every time, as do our signature sangria and daiquirís.

Our most popular drink is—you guessed it, our *cafecito*. Thousands of shots of this sweet concoction are served at our café window ("La Ventanita") each week. That little shot of sweet perfection is the key to our success, as the addictive properties of this elixir keep people coming back for more.

This chapter contains many options with which to begin, wash down, or end your delectable Cuban meal. The traditional Cuban mojito, or Hemingway's famous daiquirí are good choices. It is sacrilege to have a Cuban sandwich without a creamy mamey shake to accompany it. And a *cafecito* or *cortadito* is the crowning glory of any Cuban feast or ideal for a quick pick-me-up at any time of day or night.

Mojito

A mojito is a lime- and mint-flavored drink that has lately become very prominent. We've had this popular Cuban cocktail on our menu for decades.

Serves 1

8 fresh mint leaves, plus more for garnish
¾ ounce simple syrup (see recipe, page 152)
1 ounce fresh lime juice
1½ ounces white rum (like Bacardi®)
ice cubes
splash of sparkling or soda water
lime slices, for garnish

◈ Combine the mint and simple syrup in a cocktail shaker. Use a muddler to crush the leaves together with the simple syrup. Add the lime juice and rum, and shake well. Pour into a tall glass filled with ice. Add the sparkling water over it and garnish with slices of lime and mint leaves.

Daiquirí

The original daiquirí—made of rum, lime, and sugar—was created in Cuba in 1896 by an American mining engineer named Jennings Cox. He named the drink after the Cuban town of Daiquirí. Ernest Hemingway famously partook of this classic drink in Havana.

Serves 1

2 ounces light rum
2 teaspoons superfine sugar
1 ounce fresh lime juice
1 tablespoon Triple Sec, optional
½ cup crushed ice
1 slice lime, for garnish

◈ Combine the rum, sugar, lime juice, Triple Sec, and ice in a blender and blend for 20 to 30 seconds. Pour into a chilled glass and garnish with the lime slice. Serve immediately.

Sangria

While sangria originated in Spain, it is favored among Cubans. This recipe is simple to make and a wonderful drink for any party or get-together.

Serves 12

1 ounce brandy (preferably Spanish)
1 ounce Triple Sec
1 (750-ml) bottle red table wine
1 orange, sliced
1 lemon, sliced
½ can fruit cocktail, drained
1 ounce simple syrup (see recipe, page 152) or 3 tablespoons sugar
ice cubes
1 cup (or more to taste) lemon-lime-flavored soda

◈ Combine the brandy, Triple Sec, wine, fruit, and syrup in a large pitcher and mix well. Fill the pitcher halfway with ice cubes and top with lemon-lime soda. Serve immediately.

White Sangria

A little lighter and less sweet than the red, white sangria is a wonderful accompaniment to fish and shellfish dishes.

Serves 12

1 ounce Triple Sec
1 ounce brandy
1 ounce simple syrup (see recipe, page 152) or 3 tablespoons sugar
1 (750-ml) bottle white table wine
1 orange, sliced
1 lemon, sliced
½ can fruit cocktail, drained

ice cubes
½ cup lemon-lime-flavored soda

◈ Combine the Triple Sec, brandy, and syrup in a large pitcher. Add the wine and the fruit and mix well. Fill the pitcher halfway with ice cubes, top with lemon-lime soda, and serve immediately.

Cuban Coffee ◈ Café

Once you have Cuban coffee, it is hard to be satisfied with the thin, bitter flavor of other coffees. Cuban coffee is like hot, sweet energy in a cup. Making it is easier than you think; you just need an inexpensive aluminum stovetop espresso maker, a little elbow grease, and a little love. Measurements here are based on a 6-cup maker.

Serves 6

5 to 6 heaping teaspoons white granulated sugar (it makes the best foam)
Finely ground espresso coffee

◈ Put the sugar in a small, clean, dry metal or glass container. A measuring cup works well for this. Fill the coffee pot with water to its fill line on the side of the water receptacle. Fill the coffee receptacle with finely ground espresso coffee and lightly press it down. Place over medium-high heat with the lid open. Watch carefully. When the coffee begins to come out of the center spout, pour 1½ teaspoons of it over the sugar and return pot to the heat. With a spoon, vigorously beat the coffee and sugar mixture until smooth. It will take on a light golden color and resemble pudding in its consistency. Pour the rest of the brewed coffee into the container with the sugar and stir well. Serve immediately.

Cuban Coffee with a Shot of Milk ◈ Cortadito

The *cortadito* has always been a Cuban favorite and has become so popular in recent years that you can order it at almost any restaurant. A *cortadito* is a combination of Cuban espresso—*cafecito*—and a small amount of steamed milk. The milk is usually either whole milk or evaporated milk. At Versailles, upon request, we make it with evaporated milk, which is a little richer. Both are equally delicious and the perfect ending to any Cuban meal.

Serves 6

6 ounces whole or evaporated milk
6 ounces freshly prepared Cuban coffee
  or espresso
sugar

◈ Place milk in a small saucepan and bring to a boil (you can do this in the microwave, but it will not taste the way it should). Watch it closely as it can easily boil over. Let stand a minute or two until a film forms on top of the milk. Remove the film, pour the milk into 6 small cups, and top with coffee to desired darkness. Add sugar to taste.

Cuban Coffee with Milk ◈ Café con Leche

Café con leche is one of those things that most Cubans cannot live without—an addictive essential. Our patrons usually order it with Cuban toast and dip the bread before biting into it.

Serves 1

6 ounces whole milk
1 to 2 ounces prepared Cuban coffee
  or espresso
2 tablespoons sugar, or less depending
  on taste (some like it sweet)
small pinch salt (optional)

◈ In a small saucepan, bring the milk to a boil. Pour into a large mug and add the coffee and sugar, to taste. Add the tiniest pinch of salt, if desired.

Puffed Wheat Milk Shake ◈ Batido de Trigo

Batido de Trigo is uniquely Cuban. It is quite delicious and is made using puffed wheat cereal.

Serves 1

1 cup puffed wheat cereal
1 cup vanilla ice cream
½ cup evaporated milk
1 teaspoon sugar, or more, to taste

◈ Combine all the ingredients in a blender and blend until creamy. Pour into a tall glass and enjoy!

Mamey Milkshake ◈ Batido de Mamey

Mamey is a tropical fruit native to Mexico and Central America and also found in Cuba and Puerto Rico. It is football shaped, with a rough skin and a dense red-orange interior. Mamey is available for only a few months of the year, which is why its pulp is often sold frozen. You can find it online or in the Hispanic frozen food section of most large supermarkets.

Serves 1

1 cup vanilla ice cream
4 ounces frozen mamey pulp
¼ cup evaporated milk
1 teaspoon sugar, or more, to taste

◈ Combine all ingredients in a blender and blend until smooth and creamy. Serve immediately.

Hot Chocolate ◈ Chocolate Caliente

The perfect accompaniment to our delicious *churros*, Chocolate Caliente is a far cry from the familiar powdered hot cocoa. You will love this sinfully delicious version of the winter favorite. We like Menier® sweet chocolate, which you can find in the baking section of your grocery or where the powdered hot chocolate mixes are stocked. But if you can't find it, any sweet baking chocolate will do.

Serves 6

½ cup evaporated milk

3 tablespoons sweetened condensed milk

1 (8-ounce) bar Menier® sweet chocolate, finely chopped

3 cups whole milk

pinch of salt

sugar (optional; it's pretty sweet without extra sugar)

◈ Combine the evaporated and condensed milk in a large saucepan and bring to a boil. Immediately reduce the heat to medium-low, then add the chocolate, stirring until it melts. Whisk in the whole milk 1 cup at a time. Add the salt. Cover the pan, reduce the heat to low, and simmer for 30 minutes. Add sugar to taste.

Tip: For thicker hot chocolate, dissolve 1 teaspoon of cornstarch in ¼ cup of hot chocolate and whisk until smooth. Add this mixture to the pot little by little until combined and thickened.

Toma chocolate y paga lo que debes.

Drink chocolate and pay what you owe.*

*Suck it up.

MUCHAS GRACIAS!
Acknowledgments

From the Valls Family

To the loyal people of the best city in the world, Miami—thank you for making Versailles yours! Thank you for letting us be a part of your daily lives, for we wouldn't be here today if it weren't for you. To all of our hardworking employees—thank you for being part of the Versailles *familia*! To our loyal patrons and customers, our tourists, our online community, and the media—thank you for making Versailles the special place it is today!

From Ana

Acknowledgments are one of the hardest parts of a book to write. Whom do you thank? In what order? What if you forget someone? It's a little nerve racking, to say the least. This time it was easier. On my end the gratitude is quite simple. I feel honored to have my name on this book. I am honored to share a byline with Nicole Valls. I am humbled that the Valls family entrusted to me this important piece of their family's legacy and Miami's history.

But this is by no means my book or Nicole's book. It's really not even Versailles' book. It belongs to all of you, all of you who have graced the tables of Versailles, some for decades. It's for those of you who have entrusted your most special occasions and memories to Versailles, and for that you have our deepest thanks.

We would also like to thank Felipe Valls Sr. and Felipe Valls Jr. for bringing together their collective experience and recollections for this book. They have been a fountain of information. Researching their history and how they built an empire from the ground up has been an education in work ethic and perseverance.

To the numerous patrons, employees, and friends who endured our interrogations, thank you. Without your memories stemming from decades of experience, the pages of this book would not be as rich in history or as authentic.

Finally, to my daughters, Kati and Beba, you are the reason and the inspiration that propel everything I do. No matter how many hats I wear and how many new challenges I pursue, nothing will ever compare to the reward of being your mom.

From Nicole

I would like to thank my family for allowing me to share our story and recipes with the world—especially my dad and grandfather, my role models, whose vision for Cuban dining inspires me every day. They have instilled in me the greatest of work ethics. Through them I have been fortunate in discovering the firsthand skills, persistence, and passion required to succeed in the restaurant industry. To my mom and sisters, thank you for your support and encouragement. I am beyond grateful to be able to commission such a beautiful book on all of their behalf.

I thank Ana for all her dedication and passion spent on organizing the material and transforming our large restaurant-portioned recipes into modest single family sizes. Her understanding and knowledge of Cuban food was crucial and essential to the success of this book.

I also owe a special thanks to everyone who assisted in making this book a reality. To Jeannette Valls-Edwards and Alexandra Valls for their much appreciated, helpful, and creative edits. To Esteban Perez and José Socarras for their time and advice. Their input was instrumental in making the recipes as authentic as possible.

Versailles means so much to so many people, and I am honored that they love this restaurant as much as I do. From my grandfather's generation to future generations, our loyal customers are what we live for. So thank you and *buen provecho*!

Nicole Valls and Ana Quincoces

GLOSSARY

A caballo: Literally, "on horseback." Any dish served with two fried eggs on top.

Ajiaco: A hearty meat and vegetable stew.

Annatto: A red food coloring and flavoring used in many Latin American cuisines. It comes from the seeds of achiote trees and is a major ingredient in bijol and in the Sazón® spice blends by Goya Food.

Bijol: A seasoning and coloring condiment including annatto (from achiote tree seeds) and ground cumin; it is bright orange but turns food yellow if used more sparingly. Bijol is made by a company of the same name founded in Cuba in 1922, introduced to the United States in 1942, and operating in Miami since 1962. Substitute any annatto-based yellow coloring.

Boniato: A type of sweet potato, commonly called Cuban sweet potato.

Café con leche: Translated as "coffee with milk." A glass of Cuban coffee, or espresso, served alongside a cup of steamed milk. The coffee is poured into the milk.

Calabaza: Commonly called a Cuban squash, the calabaza is a hybrid between a pumpkin and a squash. It has green or yellow skin and yellow-orange flesh.

Chícharos: Split peas.

Chorizo: Spanish pork sausage, with a distinct red coloring that comes from paprika.

Cortadito: Translated as "short one," this is a Cuban coffee topped with steamed milk.

Croqueta preparada: A Cuban sandwich with two ham croquettes added to the inside.

Cuban bread: Bread similar to French and Italian bread, made with lard instead of oil. It has a hard, thin, almost papery crust and a soft flaky middle. It is often baked with a long, moist palm frond on top of the loaves, creating a shallow trench in the upper crust.

Cuban coffee: Espresso, to which sugar is added during the brewing process.

Fabas: Butter beans or lima beans.

Fideos: Very thin noodles, similar to vermicelli or angel hair pasta.

Frijoles colorados: Red beans.

Guava: A dense fruit with green skin and white to pink pulp. Guavas can be extremely sweet to tart, depending on their ripeness.

Jamón serrano: Spanish dry-cured ham, sliced thin, similar to Italian prosciutto.

Lacón: Smoked pork shank; a distinctive Galician-style regional product from Spain.

Lechón asado: Roasted pig.

Maduros: Fried sweet ripe plantains.

Malanga: A root vegetable, similar to taro and cassava, with a woodsy taste.

Mamey: A tropical fruit with a light pink to deep salmon pulp and a flavor of sweet pumpkin with a hint of berry.

Mariquitas: Plantain chips.

Mojo: A signature marinade of Cuba, made from garlic and sour orange juice.

Morcilla: Spanish blood pudding.

Moros: Black beans with rice, often called Moros y Cristianos (Moors and Christians).

Palomilla: Thinly cut top sirloin steak, or minute steak; a common cut of meat in Latin communities.

Picadillo: Cuban-style meat hash.

Pimentón: Smoked paprika, used to flavor Spanish chorizos and paella. It comes in three varieties—sweet and mild (*dulce*), bittersweet medium-hot (*agridulce*), and hot (*picante*).

Sabor: Flavor, taste, spirit.

Sofrito: A fragrant sauce made of garlic, onion, tomato, and bell peppers and forming the base of many Cuban dishes.

Sour orange: Also known as bitter or Seville oranges, these oranges have a very tart juice and form the basis for many Cuban marinades and sauces.

Tasajo: Salt-dried beef.

Tostones: Green or unripe plantains that are cut into slices, fried, flattened, and fried again.

Valencia rice: Valencia rice takes its name from the Valencia province of Spain. Also known as Spanish, paella, or pearl rice, this is a short-grain rice.

Vino seco: A fortified dry cooking wine that is the one exception to the "not good enough to drink, not good enough to cook with" rule. It is a must for Cuban recipes, but not the kind of wine you could ever fathom drinking. It tastes like anti-freeze but imparts a delicious and unique flavor to food.

Yuca: Also known as cassava, yuca is a starchy root similar in size and texture to the malanga. It has white flesh, a dark brown skin, and texture like a potato.

SABOR: FLAVOR, TASTE, SPIRIT.

INDEX

About Ana Quincoces

Ana Quincoces is a lawyer, author, and media personality born and raised in a Cuban household in Miami, Florida. Her mother's cooking inspired her passion for Cuban cuisine. Ana writes for several publications and is a featured chef and competitor in the South Beach Wine and Food Festival. She is a foodie-driven character on a hit Bravo nonscripted series, has cohosted ABC's *The View*, and has appeared on *The Chew* and *The Today Show*. Ana is a published author. Her books are *Cuban Chicks Can Cook* and *Sabor! A Passion for Cuban Cuisine*; her latest is in development and features slimmed-down Latin recipes. Ana recently launched her own specialty food line, Skinny Latina®; visit www.AnaQuincoces.com to learn more.

About Nicole Valls

Born and raised in Miami, Florida, Nicole Valls is the firstborn of Lourdes and Felipe Valls Jr. As the eldest of six sisters, Nicole stands as a role model to her siblings and is the first of her generation to serve in the family business. Upon graduating from the University of Miami with a bachelor of arts in business management and organization, Nicole began working full-time in various Valls Group Inc. business ventures. She has been involved with the opening of seven of her father's restaurants. She remains active in restaurant operations and is responsible for customer service, public relations, and the Valls Group charity organizations. Nicole is the vice chair of the Board of Directors of Amigos for Kids, a local nonprofit organization.

The University Press of Florida is the scholarly publishing agency for the State University System of Florida, comprising Florida A&M University, Florida Atlantic University, Florida Gulf Coast University, Florida International University, Florida State University, New College of Florida, University of Central Florida, University of Florida, University of North Florida, University of South Florida, and University of West Florida.

Pumpkin, CALABAZA, pumpkin, CALABAZA, TODO everyone EL MUNDO PA goes home.* SU CASA.

*Party's over.